Pierre Elliott Trudeau

Big Bear by Rudy Wiebe
Lord Beaverbrook by David Adams Richards
Norman Bethune by Adrienne Clarkson
Emily Carr by Lewis DeSoto
Tommy Douglas by Vincent Lam
Glenn Gould by Mark Kingwell
Louis-Hippolyte LaFontaine and Robert Baldwin
by John Ralston Saul
Wilfrid Laurier by André Pratte
Stephen Leacock by Margaret MacMillan
René Lévesque by Daniel Poliquin
Nellie McClung by Charlotte Gray
Marshall McLuhan by Douglas Coupland
L.M. Montgomery by Jane Urquhart
Lester B. Pearson by Andrew Cohen
Mordecai Richler by M.G. Vassanji
Louis Riel and Gabriel Dumont by Joseph Boyden

SERIES EDITOR:
John Ralston Saul

Pierre Elliott Trudeau
by NINO RICCI

With an Introduction by
John Ralston Saul
SERIES EDITOR

EXTRAORDINARY
CANADIANS

PENGUIN CANADA

Published by the Penguin Group

Penguin Group (Canada), 90 Eglinton Avenue East, Suite 700, Toronto,
Ontario, Canada M4P 2Y3 (a division of Pearson Canada Inc.)

Penguin Group (USA) Inc., 375 Hudson Street, New York, New York 10014, U.S.A.
Penguin Books Ltd, 80 Strand, London WC2R 0RL, England
Penguin Ireland, 25 St Stephen's Green, Dublin 2, Ireland
(a division of Penguin Books Ltd)
Penguin Group (Australia), 250 Camberwell Road, Camberwell, Victoria 3124, Australia
(a division of Pearson Australia Group Pty Ltd)
Penguin Books India Pvt Ltd, 11 Community Centre, Panchsheel Park,
New Delhi – 110 017, India
Penguin Group (NZ), 67 Apollo Drive, Rosedale, North Shore 0745, Auckland,
New Zealand (a division of Pearson New Zealand Ltd)
Penguin Books (South Africa) (Pty) Ltd, 24 Sturdee Avenue, Rosebank,
Johannesburg 2196, South Africa

Penguin Books Ltd, Registered Offices: 80 Strand, London WC2R 0RL, England

First published 2009

1 2 3 4 5 6 7 8 9 10   (RRD)

LIBRARY AND ARCHIVES CANADA CATALOGUING IN PUBLICATION

Ricci, Nino, 1959–
Pierre Elliott Trudeau / Nino Ricci.

(Extraordinary Canadians)
ISBN 978-0-670-06660-5

1. Trudeau, Pierre Elliott, 1919–2000.   2. Canada—Politics
and government—1968–1979.   3. Canada—Politics and
government—1980–1984.   4. Prime ministers—Canada—Biography.
I. Title.   II. Series: Extraordinary Canadians

FC626.T7R52 2009   971.064'4092   C2009-900461-5

Visit the Penguin Group (Canada) website at **www.penguin.ca**

Special and corporate bulk purchase rates available; please see
www.penguin.ca/corporatesales or call 1-800-810-3104, ext. 477 or 474

This book was printed on 30% PCW recycled paper

For my teachers

CONTENTS

Introduction by John Ralston Saul   IX

1   The Hero with a Thousand Faces   I

2   1968 and All That   15

3   Against the Current   47

4   *Cité libre*   89

5   Just Watch Me   109

6   In the Bedrooms of the Nation   131

7   Notwithstanding   153

8   He Haunts Us Still   183

   SOURCES   209

   ACKNOWLEDGMENTS   213

   CHRONOLOGY   217

John Ralston Saul

How do civilizations imagine themselves? One way is for each of us to look at ourselves through our society's most remarkable figures. I'm not talking about hero worship or political iconography. That is a danger to be avoided at all costs. And yet people in every country do keep on going back to the most important people in their past.

This series of Extraordinary Canadians brings together rebels, reformers, martyrs, writers, painters, thinkers, political leaders. Why? What is it that makes them relevant to us so long after their deaths?

For one thing, their contributions are there before us, like the building blocks of our society. More important than that are their convictions and drive, their sense of what is right and wrong, their willingness to risk all, whether it be their lives, their reputations, or simply being wrong in public. Their ideas, their triumphs and failures, all of these somehow constitute a mirror of our society. We look at these people, all dead, and discover what we have been, but also what we can be. A mirror is an instrument for measuring ourselves. What we see can be both a warning and an encouragement.

These eighteen biographies of twenty key Canadians are centred on the meaning of each of their lives. Each of them is very different, but these are not randomly chosen great figures. Together they produce a grand sweep of the creation of modern Canada, from our first steps as a democracy in 1848 to our questioning of modernity late in the twentieth century.

All of them except one were highly visible on the cutting edge of their day while still in their twenties, thirties, and forties. They were young, driven, curious. An astonishing level of fresh energy surrounded them and still does. We in the twenty-first century talk endlessly of youth, but power today is often controlled by people who fear the sort of risks and innovations embraced by everyone in this series. A number of them were dead—hanged, infected on a battlefield, broken by their exertions—well before middle age. Others hung on into old age, often profoundly dissatisfied with themselves.

Each one of these people has changed you. In some cases you know this already. In others you will discover how through these portraits. They changed the way the world hears music, thinks of war, communicates. They changed how each of us sees what surrounds us, how minorities are treated, how we think of immigrants, how we look after each other, how we imagine ourselves through what are now our stories.

You will notice that many of them were people of the word. Not just the writers. Why? Because civilizations are built around many themes, but they require a shared public language. So Laurier, Bethune, Douglas, Riel, LaFontaine, McClung, Trudeau, Lévesque, Big Bear, even Carr and Gould, were masters of the power of language. Beaverbrook was one of the most powerful newspaper publishers of his day. Countries need action and laws and courage. But civilization is not a collection of prime ministers. Words, words, words—it is around these that civilizations create and imagine themselves.

The authors I have chosen for each subject are not the obvious experts. They are imaginative, questioning minds from among our leading writers and activists. They have, each one of them, a powerful connection to their subject. And in their own lives, each is engaged in building what Canada is now becoming.

That is why a documentary is being filmed around each subject. Images are yet another way to get at each subject and to understand their effect on us.

The one continuous, essential voice of biography since 1961 has been the *Dictionary of Canadian Biography.* But there has not been a project of book-length biographies such as Extraordinary Canadians in a hundred years, not since the Makers of Canada series. And yet every generation understands the past differently, and so sees in the mirror of these remarkable figures somewhat different lessons. As history rolls on, some truths remain the same while others are revealed in a new and unexpected way.

What strikes me again and again is just how dramatically ethical decisions figured in these people's lives. They form the backbone of history and memory. Some of them, Big Bear, for example, or Dumont, or even Lucy Maud Montgomery, thought of themselves as failures by the end of their lives. But the ethical cord that was strung taut through their work has now carried them on to a new meaning and even greater strength, long after their deaths.

Each of these stories is a revelation of the tough choices unusual people must make to find their way. And each of us as readers will find in the desperation of the Chinese revolution, the search for truth in fiction, the political and military dramas, different meanings that strike a personal chord. At first it is that personal emotive link to such figures which draws us in. Then we find they are a key that opens the whole society of their time to us. Then we realize that in that 150-year period many of them knew each other, were friends, opposed each other. Finally, when all these stories are put together, you will see that a whole new debate has been created around Canadian civilization and the shape of our continuous experiment.

Pierre Elliott Trudeau is one of the most difficult modern figures to write about. All of us think we know him. And much of that myth of knowing has to do with how we see ourselves through the mirror of his long years of power. But knowing isn't understanding. Nino Ricci's novels have shown his great talent for revealing the complexities of the human heart. Here he has created a portrait, both psychological and intellectual, that puts together what we know with what we try to understand about Trudeau and ourselves. The strengths and weaknesses of the leader, his victories and failures, become one with the ambitions of the citizenry in an era when to be ambitious for your country—or against it—was considered the norm.

CHAPTER ONE

The Hero with a Thousand Faces

In 1967, the year of the Centennial, I was in the second grade. At school they had been handing out bronze medallions emblazoned with symbols that bore some bastard relation to the Maple Leaf, which I did not then know had only recently, and after some bitterness, replaced the Union Jack as the country's official national symbol; and they were teaching us songs that bore some even more bastard relation to "O Canada!," which I did not know would only thirteen years later, in 1980, when the song had already been in existence for a hundred years, replace "God Save the Queen" as the country's official national anthem. All I really knew was that something was afoot, something big, to judge from the fanfare, though the whole enterprise, with its funny coins and its funny songs, had a suspect air, as if there might be homework involved or extra church services.

By chance that year I came upon a teacher standing alone in the library AV room watching a news item on one of the TVs. On the screen, a man whom I remember as being in shirtsleeves was talking amid a mob scene that as a grown-up I would come to recognize as a media scrum.

The teacher had an intent look.

"That man is going to be our next prime minister," he said without taking his eyes from the screen.

I doubt I could even have said what a prime minister was at the time, let alone that we had one, and yet something not so much in the man on the TV as in the teacher's reaction to him made the moment stick with me. It was as if I had caught a glimpse of a world I had never had access to before or had witnessed a moment of jarring intimacy, in the teacher's naked, proprietary interest in someone in the news, someone on TV.

I grew up in a town where the news until then had been mainly CBS or *Time* magazine and where we rooted for the Detroit Tigers and hoped for an end to the Vietnam War. I didn't know about prime ministers, but I knew about presidents. Like much of the rest of the continent, I could remember exactly where I had been and what I'd been doing—watching the afternoon cartoons that served as my babysitter while my parents were out working on the farm—

when I'd learned that JFK had been shot. Copper memorials of Kennedy and of another late John, Pope John XXIII, hung above the dining table in our kitchen, where they seemed to set the bar for the possible both in the Old World and in the New.

It wasn't clear in this mix what being Canadian might mean. Mainly it meant what we were not: for my immigrant parents, that we didn't spend our money at the hotel the instant we earned it; for myself, that we didn't stay clean when we worked, that we picked our teeth in public, that we ate homemade bread instead of store bought. Somewhere I had got the notion that the true height of being Canadian was to be British, and I had created an alter ego for myself who went around saying things like "Pip, pip!" and "Cheerio!" in a broad English accent. But for those of us in the immigrant boonies, the murky land of Canadianness was mostly only a place we visited from time to time, the way we went into town on Friday nights to do our shopping at the A&P.

Maybe what struck me, then, in the library AV room was that simple possessive, "*our* prime minister," uttered with none of the whiff of dutifulness or exclusivity that clung, say, to events like the Centennial. The man on the TV, of course, was Pierre Trudeau, and across the country that "our" would come to take on a great deal of nuance in the years to come. For that instant, however, it was my own, as if I had suddenly sensed a different possibility than the ones represented by the two dead Johns in my family's kitchen.

AS A NOVELIST I am used to people's eyes glazing over whenever I make the mistake of trying to describe to them whatever book I'm working on. That was never the case with this particular book. Instead, at the mention of Trudeau, a certain light would come into people's eyes—wistful or philosophic or diamond hard, but a light nonetheless—and they would launch without the least preliminaries into their own personal Trudeau stories. Many of these were encounter stories of one sort or another, usually told not with the breathlessness of a celebrity spotting but in a protective tone, the way you might speak about an eccentric acquaintance whose reputation you had some share in keeping safe. But just as many involved only encounters of the mind, entirely one-sided relationships that nonetheless went on for years, through all the twists and turns—elation, anger, bitter ends and rueful relapses—of extramarital affairs. What grew clear in this was that Trudeau remained a figure with whom so many of us continued to feel a peculiar sense of engagement, as if we hadn't quite finished with him. It was also clear that this lingering connection had as much to do with what we needed to see in him as with what he was.

There are few public personages who continue even beyond the grave to spark the range of opinion Trudeau does, from the viciously demonizing to the hagiographic. He was a great man, a dilettante, a visionary, a bastard; he was a communist, he was a fascist; "the disappointment of the century" or "one of those golden beings" who walked with the gods. He was arrogant and shy, fearless and thin-skinned, generous, stingy, a maverick, and more of the same. He was "William Lyon Mackenzie King in a mini-skirt." "A political leader worthy of assassination." He was a twit. He saved the country; he tore it apart. He was a lady's man. A man's man. A boy.

A 1997 *Maclean's* survey ranked Trudeau down in the third tier of Canadian prime ministers, on par with the likes of Lester Pearson and Robert Borden. A few years earlier *The Independent* of London had given a different assessment, divvying up Canada's prime ministers into two lonely categories: "those whom the rest of the world has largely forgotten, if it ever knew about them" and Pierre Trudeau.

"I'll climb, not high perhaps," Trudeau's motto was, after Cyrano de Bergerac, "but all alone." Why, then, did so many of us follow him? One of the iconic images of Trudeau is of him dashing, suddenly, with a mischievous grin, from a flock of admirers seeking his attentions outside the Parliament Buildings. He was pushing fifty by then, a balding intellectual who had lived with his mother most of his life and who into his thirties was still seeking permission from the archbishop before reading anything on the church's index of banned books. Yet he drew us on like a rock star, with that same mix of playing to us and eluding us, seeming to speak to some need we were barely aware of until he awakened it. "Not very badly," he answered, when he was asked how much he wanted to be prime minister, and from that moment he seemed to have us eating out of his hand. We wanted him because he didn't want us, the way we wanted an unrequited love. We wanted him because we didn't know him. We wanted him because he always seemed *more:* more than met the eye, more than others had been, more than we'd hoped we could be. Because he seemed different, yet was one of us.

If he hadn't existed, we would have had to invent him. In many ways, of course, we did.

THE CLOSEST I EVER CAME TO TRUDEAU in the flesh was to stand at the back end of a crowded Toronto conference hall during the launch of one of the mostly unmemorable and unreliable summation books he was talked into ushering into print in the latter years of his life. As a child I had had the honour of second-hand contact when he reviewed the air cadet unit of one of my brothers, who reported back only that he was very short. Then in the 1980 election he caused a scandal in my hometown by agreeing to hold a rally at the upstart Lebanese Club rather than at the Italian one, something for which the Italians never forgave him, though as it happened his appearance was cancelled due to snow.

These entirely unremarkable near-misses accurately reflect, in a way, the very peripheral place that Trudeau had in my own life. Despite that glimmer of awareness in the library AV room, it is still the assassination of Robert Kennedy and not the election of Pierre Trudeau that I remember most viscerally from June 1968; if I was aware of Trudeaumania, it was with that baffled sense the young often feel at the seeming absurdity of grown-up behaviour. By the time I was dragged into anything like real political awareness, by a precocious friend who browbeat me into canvassing for the NDP in the election of 1974, the Trudeau honeymoon was long over. Soon enough even the NDP seemed entirely too establishment to me, so that I was never to vote for Trudeau or his party and was never to understand, during his reign, his two great obsessions, Quebec separatism and the constitution, the former of which seemed a matter of personal vendetta and the latter of trumped-up legacy building. And yet far more than any other Canadian public figure, Trudeau was formational for me. At no point during his regime could I have described in any detail his political philosophy or even have named, beyond his sheer persistence, his political accomplishments; yet I always felt him at my back. In this, it seems, I was not in any way distinctive but entirely typical of my generation.

Two episodes beyond my AV-room awakening stand out in my own Trudeau story as emblematic of the peculiar hold he had on me. The first occurred in the Canadian history class I took in my final year of high school, by which time Trudeau was already an overly familiar fixture on the political scene. Our teacher was one of those who had never forgiven Trudeau for the War Measures Act, but one of my fellow students presented a seminar on him that brought home to me, maybe for the first time, the irreverent iconoclast he had once seemed to the nation, a man who had caught the tail end of the communist revolution in China, who had thrown a snowball at the statue of Stalin in Red Square, who had set out for Cuba from Key West in a homemade canoe. "Citizen of the World," he'd had posted to his dorm room door at Harvard. I would discover that this high-minded sentiment was fairly common at universities, once I got to one myself, and yet I was to spend many years trying to live up to it, most of them without understanding the contradiction that lay at the heart of it. Incarnated as it was in Trudeau, the phrase seemed to hold out the possibility of being a Canadian without quite having to be one. Of being Canadian and more than Canadian. Of making the "more than," somehow, not the negation of Canadianness, but the essence of it.

The second episode took place during the summer after my first year of university, when I had in fact set out on a Trudeau-like quest across Europe using $1,500 I had left over from a student loan. The quest turned out to involve many more lonely hours waiting for rides at expressway on-ramps than I had bargained for and nowhere near as much enlightenment or sex, but along the way there were those few special moments when the reality came breathtakingly close to the fantasy. One occurred in Norway. I had had a hellish time with mosquitoes and rain in the north of Sweden looking for the midnight sun, but then I had entered into God's country, coming down through Norway across stunning mountains and fjords that went on in endless succession.

I had caught a ride with a kindly young pastor moving house from north to south.

"I would like to visit one day to your side," he said, "but of course it is always the U.S. I think to come to, not so much Canada."

Who could blame him, really? Canada the quaint. Canada the forgotten.

He dropped me on the Oslo road. The next car that pulled up—in my idealized memory of the event it is a convertible, and the top is down, and the Norwegian air is pellucid under a brilliant northern sun—turned out to be the dream ride, the sort every hitchhiking male prayed for but never got: five Norwegian blondes, and not the quiet, mousy, world-shy ones of the mountains but the feisty, progressive blondes of the south. I was packed into the backseat between two of them, where I felt utterly overwhelmed. Then came the inevitable question, where was I from, and my squeaky reply.

"Canada! How wonderful!"

It was as if I had come from Valhalla, to tell them the news from the other side. What they wanted to know about: Maggie and Pierre. So this was the sort of tabloid gossip it took to be known in the world, to have a bit of cachet. Back home, of course, the whole sordid affair had already passed from the merely tawdry to the downright embarrassing. Yet even in my disdain there was a pride, a sense of affirmation:

I came from a place of sufficient complexity to have a scandal of international proportions. It was like wearing genuine Levis, say, instead of the BiWay knock-offs I'd had to wear as a kid. The difference between holding your own and non-existence.

"We don't pay that much attention to them anymore," I said lightly, riding the high of my celebrity for days afterwards even though I'd been dropped not five miles down the road when the girls reached their turnoff.

IT WAS ONE OF THE PARADOXES of Trudeau, the anti-nationalist, that he brought to so many Canadians a sense of national identity they could finally live with. In some way he spoke to the contradictions at the heart of us, to our being this nation of many nations that often felt like no nation at all—one that barely had its own flag or its own song, that still looked to London and Paris and New York for its culture and to Washington for its politics. A place that was "not so much a country," as Mordecai Richler once put it, "as a holding tank filled with the disgruntled progeny of defeated peoples."

None of these propositions was quite as true after Trudeau's reign as before it. As much as anything, this shift in our collective self-perception was a matter of style. From the moment

Trudeau appeared on Parliament Hill in his Mercedes roadster it was clear something had changed: here was a man who seemed afraid of nothing, who went his own way, who had none of the cultural cringe that was the Canadian norm. It has always been an open question, of course, how much of that style flowed naturally from him and how much of it was strategic. His "Not very badly" of 1968 looks a little disingenuous next to the ample evidence in his archive that he had been honing himself for politics from a young age. Trudeau was not the sort to stint when he set himself an objective. Sickly and weak by disposition as a child, he turned himself into a superb athlete; shy in crowds, he sharpened his debating skills and became a formidable orator. Far from having been dragged into political leadership, he seemed to have been training for it all his life, perfecting his talents with the precision of a master craftsman. This coldly calculated version of Trudeau doesn't quite square with Trudeau the gunslinger, the man who spoke his mind, yet the calculation was there, perhaps not so much as one makes an object for some specific use but as one makes art, including flourishes for their own sake. There is that aspect to Trudeau's life, when it is read in full, the sense of a man with the leisure and means—would that we all had them—to consciously fashion his life as one might fashion a work of art.

Works of art are about much more than style, of course. They are about style in the service of content, or more correctly about style as content, about the point where the two merge. Style, really, is what makes it possible for art to be art, to hold a hundred balls in the air without dropping any, to contain in a single package unresolvable contradictions— and the really good contradictions are the unresolvable ones—without splitting apart at the seams. Trudeau was nothing if not a package of contradictions. The anglophone French Canadian. The woodsy sophisticate. The rich socialist. The passionate man of reason. Follow any thread of his life and you inevitably end up in some paradox. The fierce advocate for human rights who went spearfishing with dictators. The devout Roman Catholic who took buggery off the law books, gave us no-fault divorce, and laid the ground for abortion on demand. And yet, like a successful work of art, he hung together. There was a wholeness to him that we looked to, and a breadth of character that gave sanction to our own contradictions, and our own hopes.

While doing the research for this book I often felt as I did a few years ago doing research for a novel on the life of Jesus: that I had stepped into a war zone of vested interests and scholarly bloodletting, with no opinion unpartisan or untainted. Interestingly, Jesus, like Trudeau—though I wouldn't want to carry this analogy too far—was another of history's contradiction-bridgers, surely one of the reasons his story has had such staying power. That is the fate of some stories: they speak so deeply to our hopes and fears, to the disjunctions of our lives and our wish to overcome them, that they pass from art to myth.

Michael Valpy, describing myth as what "reveals the deep patterns of meaning and coherence in a culture," what "shows us who we dream ourselves to be," has made the argument for Trudeau as "our one truly mythological prime minister." There remain legions of dissenters, however, particularly in Quebec and in the West, who still grow apoplectic at such appraisals, and for whom the only proper application of the term *myth* to the Trudeau legacy is in the sense of unholy fiction, of a great lie perpetrated on the Canadian people. Even here the contradictions repeat themselves, for the more we learn of Trudeau, the more those two opposing summations of him seem inextricably intertwined.

CHAPTER TWO

1968 and All That

Nineteen sixty-eight was one of those watershed years in human history that was almost enough to make even the most cynical believe in astrological forces. In France it was the year of May '68; in Poland, of March '68; in the United States, of Chicago '68. It was the year of the Prague Spring. Of bra burning. Of *Hair*.

In Canada we tend to look at 1967's Expo as the evidence that we, too, even before Trudeau arrived on the scene, had been moving toward our own '68. Thinking of Expo 67 as a precursor to the spirit of 1968, however, is a bit like thinking of Sunday school as a proper warm-up for a Grateful Dead concert. In the United States, in 1967, they had the Summer of Love: tens of thousands of youths descending on Haight-Ashbury from around the world with flowers in their hair and sex and drugs and rock 'n' roll on their minds. All this was a far cry from the official government ditties of Expo and its images of happy families and of high-end futurist real estate. The Summer of Love was a sort of pollination event for 1968, sending its converts back out into the world to spread the good news about turning on and dropping out, though it was also a warning of the ephemeral nature of hippie ideals, quickly deteriorating into a sordid scene of crime, souvenir hawking, and drugs.

Most of us have learned by now to hang our heads in shame at the memory of hippie drug culture, though it may have been that hippies were merely self-medicating to dull the pain of forever banging their heads against the status quo. What we often forget is that in the short term, at least, the real story of 1968 was as much about the crushing suppression of the human spirit as about its assertion: in France, the massive protests gave way to betrayals and backroom deals that ended in the re-election of the Gaullists, stronger than ever; in Czechoslovakia, two hundred thousand Warsaw Pact troops turned the Prague Spring into a Soviet winter. In China, one of the last hopes of Western Marxists after the disappointment of Stalin, 1968 was the year that Mao's take on counterculture, the Cultural Revolution, completed its pendulum swing back to iron-fisted tyranny after leading the country to the brink of chaos. Meanwhile the United States saw the assassination of Martin Luther King; the assassination of Robert Kennedy; and finally the election of that great standard-bearer of 1960s radicalism, Richard Nixon. Even bra burning, often cited as the inaugural moment of second-wave feminism, has been overbilled: the term arose after a smattering of protesters outside the 1968 Miss America pageant in Atlantic City dumped bras, girdles, and various other symbols of women's oppression into a trash can, though the suggestion of setting fire to them was swiftly quashed by local police. On television sets across the nation, meanwhile, the Miss America pageant carried on uninterrupted.

Around the world, then, the most immediate outcome of 1968's sudden flourishing of a new order was the brutal reaffirmation of the old one. Next to this titan clash of cosmic forces, an event like Expo 67 begins to seem, well, decidedly Canadian. Expo was not about counterculture but about Culture, with a very capital *C*—about claiming we actually had one. It wasn't about taking down the Establishment but about establishing one.

"Now for me in those years," journalist Rick Salutin has written, "what has since become a great icon of Canadian potential—Expo 67—signified nothing." Salutin, back then, had done what any proper Canadian radical needed to do: he had left the country. "But Trudeau," Salutin goes on, "—mere news reports about him—moved me."

This is a remarkable statement coming from someone who was hobnobbing at the time with the Maoists and Fidelistas of the New Left down in Harlem and Washington Square. If Expo was no logical place to look for the spirit of 1968, then one would hardly have expected to find it in the Liberal Party of Canada, whose front man until then, Lester Pearson, was considered too boring and nice even by mainstream Canadians. When Pearson announced his retirement at the end of 1967, the principal contenders for his job were people like Paul Martin Sr. and Robert Winters and Mitchell Sharp, who were as establishment and staid a group of stuffed shirts as you could poke a fickle finger of fate at.

In this pack, Trudeau's candidacy initially seemed a kind of joke. Here was someone whose only connection to the federal Liberals before 1965 had been to poke vicious fun at them in the pages of his magazine *Cité libre*. In 1963 he had taken particular aim at Pearson, a Nobel Peace Prize laureate, referring to him as "the defrocked prince of peace" for allowing American nuclear warheads on Canadian soil. Yet a mere two years later he had stood for election as a Liberal MP, and within weeks of arriving in Ottawa was serving as Pearson's parliamentary secretary. Back in Quebec, Trudeau's only involvement in party politics until then, apart from a brief flirtation with the NDP's predecessor, the CCF, had been in ad hoc leftist movements and coalitions that he had quickly lost interest in or that had self-destructed. To many of his old political colleagues in Quebec—people like Claude Ryan and René Lévesque, with whom he had been allied in the fight against the corrupt regime of Maurice Duplessis—Trudeau's defection to Ottawa seemed so much a departure from any of his previous leanings that they were left dumbfounded.

As with many of Trudeau's seemingly cavalier gestures, there was probably a lot more calculation in his jump to the Liberals than met the eye. Yet it is almost certain he would not have made it—and hence that none of what happened to him in the crucial next three years would have come about—if he had merely been left to follow his own inclinations. Despite the image that has come down to us of Trudeau as the loner, as the one who followed his own road, at almost every crucial juncture in his life there was some significant figure whose influence over him was definitive. Looked at in this light, his meteoric rise begins to seem neither the happenstance event it was often played as at the time nor the coldly calculated one it was later suspected of being. Rather, Trudeau seems to have been urged toward his path by the people around him almost despite himself, as if they saw more clearly than he did that some mark of destiny lay on him, that the moment would come when no one but he could draw the sword from the stone.

One man whose role it would be hard to overestimate in this period was Jean Marchand. Marchand, a union organizer and populist with tremendous street credibility in Quebec, was the real star the Liberals were after in 1965, in a desperate bid to rebuild their Quebec base after several of the more prominent Liberals there—always a touchy subject in Quebec—had fallen to scandals. Marchand had first met Trudeau during the Asbestos Strike of 1949, when the young Trudeau, to Marchand's chagrin, had fired up the striking miners with revolutionary rhetoric as if he were preaching to his schoolmates rather than to men who had access to dynamite, and the will to use it. Nonetheless, Marchand had been struck by the ability of this citified member of the elite to speak to uneducated workers in terms they understood. He had kept up only sporadic contact with Trudeau in the intervening years, but when the Liberals approached Marchand in 1965 to head their Quebec team, he refused to sign on unless he was allowed to bring with him his friend Gérard Pelletier, then the editor of *La Presse,* and, somewhat bafflingly, Pierre Trudeau.

Somehow Marchand managed not only to talk the Liberals into accepting Trudeau—this was a man who not long before had publicly condemned them as imbeciles and trained donkeys—but to talk Trudeau into accepting the Liberals. Trudeau was apparently in high spirits after agreeing to run, as if he were merely setting out on another of his great adventures. But he was to falter many times along the road, and each time it was Marchand who set him back on course. It was Marchand who talked him out of running in the rural riding of his ancestors and wrangled a safe urban one for him, the upscale and largely anglophone Mount Royal; it was Marchand who convinced him to stay in the race when Trudeau discovered he would be up against his old friend, the philosopher Charles Taylor, who was running for the NDP. Then in Ottawa, when Trudeau initially turned down the offer to serve as Pearson's parliamentary secretary—as it happened, Trudeau was on a ski trip in the Alps when Pearson reached him—Marchand was on the phone to him at once. In the memoirs Trudeau published in 1993, he recalled Marchand's reprimand: "What brought us here is that there's a job to be done, and we have to grab every opportunity to do it." One suspects that Marchand's actual terms were a bit more colourful.

Marchand, it seemed, had Trudeau's number, spurring him forward with a mix of coaxing and bullying that might have reminded Trudeau of another significant male in his life, his father, Charles. Charles Trudeau, who died of hard living when Pierre was fifteen, had been in the habit of weeding out weakness from his son by challenging him to overcome it. In the first grade, for instance, when Pierre complained of a problem with his teacher, Charles refused to intervene, sending the shy young Pierre off to the school principal to solve the matter himself. The strategy worked: Trudeau proved so successful at meeting these challenges that they became a sort of addiction, each one emboldening him for the next until he came to seek out anything that smacked of a dare. Jean Marchand somehow understood this side of Trudeau and learned how to use it, goading him again and again into actions that flew in the face of the expected but that clearly had an appeal for Trudeau precisely for that reason. It made sense, as historian John English suggests in the first volume of his two-volume biography of Trudeau, *Citizen of the World,* that Trudeau would balk at accepting an offer from Pearson that would have him working so closely with a man he hardly knew and had never much liked. But once Marchand framed the job as a challenge, Trudeau embraced it wholeheartedly. Marchand, with shrewd pre-science, foresaw great things for Trudeau, predicting to a Quebec colleague in Ottawa just after the election that Trudeau would be the Liberals' "big man in French Canada" within a year, "eclipsing all the others."

The other person who may have had Trudeau's number was Pearson himself. Marchand had asked Pearson to give Trudeau some sort of position that would bring him in from the back benches, but it was Pearson's idea to take Trudeau into his own office. A ministry would have been a mistake, not just because of Trudeau's inexperience but because of the resentment still simmering against him in the rest of the caucus. But it was an act of some magnanimity on Pearson's part to take as his aide a man who had so roundly pilloried him in his writings. It couldn't have helped much that Trudeau's "defrocked prince of peace" line—like several of the famous lines history has attributed to Trudeau—was one he had merely quoted from another writer. Yet Pearson, who had actually given as one of his reasons for choosing Trudeau as a candidate that he had always been impressed by his writings, had clearly decided well before Trudeau arrived in Ottawa that he would be an invaluable asset. It is often overlooked that the two major accomplishments we tend to associate with Trudeau—bilingualism and constitutional reform—grew out of initiatives he inherited from Pearson, who seemed to have understood better than most the formidable talents that Trudeau could bring to bear on them.

Trudeau expected to be put off in his new job with "some modest parliamentary chores and some pencil pushing."

Instead Pearson immediately sent him on missions to Paris and the U.N. and to the countries of the fledgling Francophonie, where he hobnobbed with such post-colonial heroes of the day as President Léopold Senghor of Senegal and Habib Bourguiba of Tunisia. It is hard not to suspect an element of cunning in all this on Pearson's part. Not only was Trudeau exactly the sort of sophisticate to send to places like Paris and to a poet-president like Senghor, but these missions had the added advantage of giving Trudeau an international profile—and a rather more statesmanlike one than that of Trudeau the vagabond from the less official travels of his youth—while keeping him out of the line of fire of the people gunning for him back in Ottawa.

Early in 1967, after some fifteen months of globetrotting, Trudeau got the call to come home. In the meantime Marchand and Pearson had been busy, clearing Cabinet of deadwood from the Quebec caucus, so that by April Pearson was able to offer Trudeau the justice ministry. By now Trudeau was fully in the game. He didn't hesitate for a second, as he later put it, but went straight to the department's top bureaucrats to get up to speed.

For most Canadians it was as justice minister that Trudeau first came to their attention. He took over the portfolio a rank outsider, known mainly as a playboy and a maverick and taken seriously only by the observant few; within a matter of months he would have national prominence and an aura of authority most politicians had to build over the course of years. Much of his rapid rise had to do with a decision he made only days after taking over his portfolio. For some time, legislation updating the country's divorce laws and various controversial sections of the Criminal Code had been languishing in committee for lack of political will to push it through. "You're a novice minister," the civil servants said to Trudeau, in his version of events, "so perhaps it would be better to start with a less thorny issue." But Trudeau, ever the contrarian, said, "No. I prefer to start with the most difficult one."

It was a fateful choice. By late December 1967, the Criminal Code amendments—which, among other changes, decriminalized homosexuality and contraception and legalized abortion under certain conditions—had been cleaned up and introduced in the House. Suddenly Trudeau was in the national spotlight, receiving accolades from every corner for tackling issues no one else had dared to saddle themselves with. This would later appear to be the moment when Trudeau finally came into his own, outstripping expectations and justly earning his political stripes. Yet once again there is the question of how much he seized the moment and how much he was manoeuvred toward it. The legislation itself, the product of many hands and of years of hard-won consensus, Trudeau could hardly take much credit for; all it had required was the right man to push it through. One can almost imagine that Pearson, taking a page from Marchand, had actually instructed the bureaucrats to warn Trudeau off of it, knowing that Trudeau would surely go for it then. In any event, whether by fluke or by calculation, Pearson had once more put Trudeau exactly where he needed to be. It may have been no coincidence that only days before the legislation was introduced Pearson had announced that he would be retiring the following spring, so that almost at once people began bandying Trudeau's name around for a possible leadership bid, a prospect that would have seemed fanciful even a few weeks earlier.

As much as anything, it had been Trudeau's way with the *mot juste* that had made such a coup of his legislation. In the media scrum following the introduction of the bill, he had staked his claim on the country's imagination with the line "There's no place for the state in the bedrooms of the nation." It was a brilliant phrase, one that fit perfectly the spirit of the times, and that so much came to embody the public image of Trudeau as forward-thinking and clear-headed and no-nonsense that over the years even Trudeau himself seemed to forget that he had more or less cribbed it from an editorial earlier that week in *The Globe and Mail*. No one in the media seems to have caught the borrowing at the time. No matter: Trudeau, quite literally, had made the phrase his own. Nor did the media take the trouble to parse its tacit reference to the removal of sodomy from the Criminal Code: an entirely laudable change, and long overdue, but one that might not have played so well to the general public of the day if it had been spelled out in all its specificity. Instead, journalists, by and large, took the high road, branding Trudeau a gifted phrasemaker and essentially setting the stage for his leadership bid.

Perhaps Trudeau had merely caught the media on a good day. What seems truer, however, is that if people like Marchand and Pearson were quietly urging Trudeau toward the starry crown, then the media, at least in English Canada, were waiting to place it on his head. Peter Gzowski's portrait of Trudeau in *Maclean's* back in 1962 had set the tone for the English take on Trudeau, presenting him as the angry young Renaissance man, equal parts athlete and connoisseur and *engagé* intellectual. Aspects of Trudeau that his acquaintances in Quebec had always regarded as signs of a certain dilettantism were thus transformed into parts of a complete, well-integrated package. Over the next years Trudeau was to attract a growing fan club in English Canada that included journalists like Peter Newman and Pierre Berton and intellectuals like historian Ramsay Cook and media guru Marshall McLuhan.

An episode of CBC-TV's *Newsmagazine* that aired in May 1967, just after Trudeau's appointment as justice minister and months before he had risen to anything like national prominence, was typical of Trudeau coverage of the time. It began with what was then a common slip, knocking three years off Trudeau's age to put him at forty-four instead of forty-seven, and called him "one of the younger cabinet ministers in our history," though Jean Chrétien and John Turner, appointed to Cabinet at the same time as Trudeau, were both much younger (Turner thirty-seven and Chrétien a mere stripling at thirty-three). The interviewer, a very fatherly looking Norman DePoe, then made a slightly tortured connection between Trudeau and Sir John A. Macdonald, as if to establish a sacred lineage. Much of the interview that followed, under the guise of dredging up some of the shadows dogging Trudeau's appointment—his inexperience, his unconventional opinions, his questionable past—was merely a set-up for Trudeau to make humbly manifest his wide experience and his wide learning.

Well along, DePoe paused to ask the very question that his viewers might have been asking themselves: "Why a program about Trudeau rather than some other equally new and equally promising cabinet minister?" There followed a lengthy resumé that presented Trudeau as "the first real chance for the turned-on generation to have a real voice in national affairs," and that gave Trudeau's status as "a rebel and a swinger" equal weight with his impressive life experience and his academic credentials (in addition to his law degree, "higher degrees" from Harvard, the Sorbonne, and the London School of Economics were mentioned, though Harvard was the only one of these institutions Trudeau ever actually graduated from). The summary performed the by then familiar gestalt of transforming a past full of the sorts of gaps and incompletions that would have prevented most people from landing decent jobs into a well-balanced, scintillating whole. The encomium ended thus: "Most of all, though, he cares."

Fawning might not have been the right word for this sort of treatment: DePoe was intelligent throughout, he asked difficult questions, he showed an understanding both of the times and of history. His tone, however, was manifestly paternal, as if he had found a promise for the future and was helping Trudeau along his path. Trudeau was playing his part, the humble servant of the Crown, yet the impression the interview leaves now across the distance of years is that it was not so much either Trudeau or DePoe who were in control as some outside force, some bigger narrative the camera was merely the instrument of.

A coda to the piece went on to make the obligatory references to Trudeau's impressive athleticism and way with the ladies—"Trudeau, the bachelor sports car driver, frequently escorts some of the most ornamental and intelligent women around, and for him they must be intelligent"—and then ended with a question that would have seemed strange at the outset but by now had an air of inevitability: "Do you want to be prime minister some day?" Trudeau, sheepish, answered with a "Hell, no" that was delivered not quite as believably, perhaps, as the "Not very badly" of his leadership campaign many months later. Yet he seemed sufficiently flattered by the question to suggest that there was still the innocence in him of someone who would never have believed he would be sitting in the prime minister's office in less than a year.

Whatever Trudeau's later, much more fractious relationship with the media, in English Canada at this point he could do no wrong, as journalists like DePoe lined up behind Trudeau's other father figures to push Trudeau forward as the favoured son. Writer and editor George Galt has pointed out that what these journalists were probably feeling was relief: here, finally, was someone like them. Trudeau had been formed not in the political backrooms but in the journalistic trenches, having cut his teeth in the 1950s writing the sort of no-holds-barred political commentary that represented exactly the ideals many of these journalists aspired to. The prospect of such a man holding political leadership must have seemed a tantalizing one to them, as if they themselves were the ones acceding to power.

Trudeau's media profile in Quebec was more complex. He had already had a substantial media presence there before entering politics, and couldn't play the young ingenue unaware of his own powers or count on the rosy lens of half-knowledge to hide his blemishes. His defection to Ottawa had embittered many of his former allies in Quebec's increasingly nationalistic elite, the very people who, after the death of Duplessis, had taken control not only of Quebec's political machinery but of its media. Now that Trudeau was a declared federalist, any pronouncement from him, particularly on the French question, was greeted either skeptically or with scorn. It was still a protective scorn, however, the scorn reserved for one of their own, underlain with a grudging pride in this man who had stepped boldly among the English wolves and was being taken seriously by them. Trudeau's contention that he had gone to Ottawa to show that Quebecers "could play with the big boys," though it had a typically cavalier ring to it, actually touched on one of the deep insecurities underlying Quebec nationalism: the fear of not being able to "make it" outside the safe confines of home. That was really what lay at the heart of Trudeau's by now vehement rejection of the nationalists: the perception—almost unique to him at the time—that their increasing sway under the Quiet Revolution was merely a continuation by other means of the insularity and narrow-mindedness of Duplessis's "Great Darkness."

Ironically, Trudeau's Criminal Code legislation, which would have been anathema under the old, church-based Quebec nationalism of Trudeau's youth, actually played well in the new, post–Quiet Revolution Quebec. The province had so long been under the yoke of the Catholic Church that when it broke with it, it did so precipitously, quickly moving from being one of the most priest-ridden societies on earth to being one of the most secular. Despite an outcry from the church establishment, Trudeau's reforms struck a responsive chord in the province, particularly in the cities and among the educated elite. In the media the emphasis was much less on the man behind the bill than on the bill itself, with round-table discussions on the social issues it raised and soul-searching documentaries on subjects like the marginalization of homosexuals. Yet for Trudeau the timing, again, was ideal: here was a bill that compromised none of his own political beliefs and yet fit in perfectly with the agenda of the new nationalists, who may even have been grateful for this chance to show their approval of their native son without seeming to. In any event it could not have been lost on Quebecers that it had taken someone from home, from the traditionally "backward" province, to bring the rest of Canada out of the Dark Ages.

WHEN TRUDEAU ANNOUNCED his candidacy for the leadership of the Liberal Party on February 16, 1968—he was the last to do so, a mere month and a half before the convention, though at a point when Trudeaumania was already in full swing—he told reporters that they were to blame for his decision. They had started what they had thought was "a huge practical joke on the Liberal Party," he said, daring the Liberals to choose someone as unconventional as himself as their leader, and had ended up being taken seriously. Given the amount of backroom strategizing that we now know preceded Trudeau's announcement, his depicting his run as a kind of accident comes across as somewhat disingenuous. Already over the Christmas break, not two weeks after Pearson had announced his resignation and while Trudeau himself was vacationing in Tahiti and meeting the girl who would eventually become his wife, a few choice associates back home had begun secretly organizing for his potential candidacy. Still, he might never have put himself forward if the various forces urging him on hadn't reached a kind of crescendo in the first weeks of 1968.

The crucial push came, again, from Marchand. He was the one from the start whom the Liberals had been thinking of as a credible successor to Pearson, to keep up the Liberal tradition of alternating English- and French-Canadian leaders. But Marchand hadn't taken to Ottawa. His health was failing; he was known to imbibe. "It's a crazy job," he had told his friend André Laurendeau, co-chair of the Royal Commission on Bilingualism and Biculturalism, "worse even than being a trade unionist—there at least you've got roots." Unlike Trudeau, Marchand hadn't quite been able to leave home. In particular, he didn't "like to speak English all the time; it diminishes me by fifty per cent."

Early in the new year, Marchand, Trudeau, and Gérard Pelletier, who had set off together for Ottawa little more than two years earlier, met in Montreal at the Café Martin. "The Three Wise Men," they had been dubbed in English Canada at the time, though in Quebec, somewhat less charitably, they were known as *Les trois colombes,* "The Three Doves." Marchand had remained their front man and strategist, though now, over dinner, he told the others that he would not run for the Liberal leadership. Trudeau had surely suspected this change of heart by then. Six months earlier Marchand had even taken the line that the francophones shouldn't run any candidate at all, since the current nationalist climate in Quebec would inevitably cast any francophone leader as a mere apologist for the English. But Trudeau must also have suspected that it had surely crossed Marchand's mind more than once to put Trudeau himself forward as a candidate, particularly in the weeks since his Criminal Code bill, given the frequency with which that suggestion had been cropping up in the national media.

According to Pelletier, however, Trudeau was "stunned" when Marchand presented exactly this option. Whether he was actually stunned or only strategically so we will never know: by this point, when people were already working behind the scenes to set up a campaign office for him, Trudeau had entered into the kind of cat-and-mouse game he was so good at, growing more deferential and coy the more people insisted. The historical consensus, in any event, is that Trudeau would surely never have run if Marchand had chosen to, and his seeming shock at Marchand's proposal may have been simply the realization that his candidacy was no longer just a kind of intellectual game but a real possibility. In later life, Trudeau admitted that he had often appeared most cavalier about the things he'd been most afraid of failing at, and this may have been one of those moments, never seen publicly, when his reach suddenly came up against his fear.

Trudeau's strategy of deferral, in this regard, had one huge advantage: he could walk away at any moment with no loss of face. Another advantage was that the longer he remained uncommitted, the more he was plied with inducements. Pearson, who was determined he would be the country's last unilingual prime minister, offered a large one: he arranged for Trudeau, as justice minister, to set out on a country-wide series of talks with the provincial premiers in preparation for a constitutional conference in early February. Thus, while the other leadership candidates were busy with the petty nuts and bolts of their campaigns, Trudeau stood above the fray, dominating the media day after day as he travelled the country and completely eclipsing the leadership race. At each stop he acquired new fans, including such unlikely allies as the fabled Newfoundland premier Joey Smallwood and British Columbia's long-standing Social Credit premier, "Wacky" William Bennett.

Trudeau, however much the issue was to become a defining one for him, had initially been opposed to the constitutional talks. The constitution, he had said, with more foresight than he could have known, was "a can of worms" that would be hard to close again once opened. But now he rose to this challenge as he had to the others that had been put before him, with a confidence and a level of expertise that must have surprised all the fusty old-school politicians on the Hill who had initially dismissed him as a mere showman. The crowning moment came at the constitutional conference itself, which Trudeau dominated, outlining the federalist option in clear and precise terms and completely outshining Quebec premier Daniel Johnson. By now Trudeau was exactly where he wanted—and needed—to be: though he had yet to declare himself a candidate there was a groundswell of opinion for him to do so, though a scant two months before, as Trudeau himself noted wryly, the idea of his candidacy had never been mentioned.

In this mix it is hard to sort out what was cunning on Trudeau's part and what was luck, what was people imagining in Trudeau what they wanted to see and what was really there. Given all the behind-the-scenes machinations that went into placing Trudeau just so in the spotlight, the idea that he simply burst on the scene out of nowhere through the sheer force of his charisma doesn't hold up. But neither does the argument that he had been calculating his rise from the start. Already from his nomination meeting in Mount Royal back in 1965 Trudeau had been prepared to bow out in favour of his one opponent, Victor Goldbloom, who was a "good man," he'd said, and surely deserved the nomination as much as Trudeau himself did. Whatever strategy there may have been in this oft-repeated habit of playing the reluctant bride, what made it effective was that Trudeau was clearly bloody-minded enough to walk away from the prize without regrets if he couldn't get it on his own terms. He had to be cajoled; he had to be convinced; he had to be kept to the path. Without a Marchand next to him, goading him on, or a Pearson or a Norman DePoe, he might simply have strapped on his skis and hit the slopes.

The rest, as they say, is history. Trudeaumania, already in full swing by the end of the constitutional conference, seemed only to grow more fervent. It managed to carry Trudeau through the leadership convention in April and two months later through the election, where he won the majority that had always eluded Pearson. If anything, what seemed surprising in retrospect was that it had taken four ballots for him to win the leadership, and that if some of those candidates who bitterly opposed him had been smart enough to consolidate their support behind one of his rivals, he wouldn't have won it at all. On the convention floor,

Secretary of State Judy LaMarsh, not realizing the cameras were on her, pleaded with Paul Hellyer to withdraw and throw his support behind Robert Winters. "What's the point of going down and letting that bastard be there?" she said. But the bastard won.

There was one Liberal stalwart whose allegiance wasn't in doubt, however. While Lester Pearson, as was appropriate, had kept up a look of judicious impartiality during the convention, allowing himself only the merest smile at the final numbers, his wife, Maryon, clearly smitten, couldn't suppress her glee.

IN RETROSPECT, despite the serious aberration that Trudeaumania was from the country's usual habits, the whole phenomenon took on an air of inevitability, as if exactly what should have happened, had. But what had actually happened? A collective delusion, of the same sort that put demagogues in power? Or, seen more positively, a coming of age, a willingness to take risks, to bet, in Trudeau's words, "on the new guys with new ideas"? For a moment, at any rate, our aspirations seemed incarnated before us in the flesh. Not a very long moment, as it happened. "Good Will for Trudeau, for a Time," a *Toronto Telegram* headline read after the convention. For Maryon Pearson, the bloom went off the Trudeau rose within a couple of weeks. While she had been able to forgive Trudeau his jibes at her husband in the pages of *Cité libre,* she couldn't forgive him the short shrift he gave Pearson after his leadership win, when, among other slights, he dissolved Parliament for the election before the House had had a chance to give Pearson the traditional tribute accorded to outgoing leaders.

In any event, he didn't have much need of Pearson after his leadership win: the crowds were mobbing him, women were kissing him in the streets, and the media was lapping it all up. Not everyone, of course, was on side. Despite the unprecedented level of interest in Trudeau, the election in June wasn't exactly a rout. Although the Liberal popular vote rose by some 5 percent—a massive shift as far as winning seats was concerned—most of the gain was at the expense not of the main opposition parties, which held fairly steady, but of the Alberta-inspired Social Credit Party, which more or less disappeared at the time, only to resurface years later as the Reform Party after Trudeau had left the scene. What the numbers indicate, perhaps, is that however captivated Canadians were by Trudeau, they weren't ready to give away the farm. From the start, in fact, the interest in Trudeau had as much to do with the fervour of his detractors as with that of his supporters.

Stephen Clarkson and Christina McCall, in their seminal work *Trudeau and Our Times,* looked at Trudeaumania through the lens of sociologist Max Weber's theories of charisma. Trudeau, in their view, presented the classic features of a political charismatic: a certain foreignness and a "sexual mystique," among other qualities, but "above all, an extraordinary calling or vocation and along with it, the fighting stance of the crusader preaching social change." For Clarkson and McCall, however, the Trudeau charisma was a mask hiding a reality that fell far short of the image. Marshall McLuhan had also taken note of the Trudeau mask, though his own, koanlike pronouncements on it sounded entirely approving. "This is your 'cool' TV power," he wrote to Trudeau after watching one of the televised leaders' debates. "Iconic, sculptural. A mask 'puts on' an audience. At a masquerade we are not private persons."

Whether we see it as a lie or a skill, a useful illusion or dangerous deception, Trudeau's mask did indeed become many things to many people during his rise, tapping into a sudden desire or need for a hero in a country generally better at burying its heroes than raising them up. Joseph Campbell's *The Hero with a Thousand Faces,* which traces the basic narrative underlying most hero stories, may give us a framework for understanding the Trudeau phenomenon to put next to Max Weber's.

> A hero ventures forth from the world of common day into a region of supernatural wonder: fabulous forces are there encountered and a decisive victory is won: the hero comes back from this mysterious adventure with the power to bestow boons on his fellow man.

Trudeau was the man who had studied at Harvard and the Sorbonne, who had caught the tail end of Mao's revolution, who had travelled the world and ridden the white charger and wooed the fair maidens. Who had won the decisive victory and would bring home the boons, promised to us in what he called the Just Society.

The Just Society. Trudeau, the great phrase-poacher, likely cadged this one from his former mentor F.R. Scott or from Plato, who had served Trudeau well more than once on the campaign trail. His first use of the phrase during the Liberal leadership convention had seemed a stab in the dark, as if he had been reaching for something loftier, something at the level of LBJ's Great Society, and had come up with only this slightly lame undergraduate substitute. Yet the phrase caught on. Over the years the Just Society would come to consist of whatever policy the Trudeau Liberals happened to be pushing that day, but at the outset what seemed to matter was the tone it caught rather than any specifics, how it seemed to join a Bob Dylanesque sense of changing times with the more traditional "peace, order, and good government" of something made in Canada.

That, perhaps, beyond his Weberian charisma or his Campbellian heroism, was the truly bewitching thing about Trudeau for Canadians: he was made in Canada. The contradictions he resolved were *our* contradictions. For both anglophones and francophones, he seemed a model of being oneself and yet more than oneself, of being Canadian in a way that wasn't defined by negatives. For immigrants, meanwhile, and for all those in the grey zone of the not-quite-included, he was the end of an old boys' WASP hegemony, the man who rose from the outside to the top.

It would take some doing to sort out all the ways we were wrong about Trudeau in those first heady days, just as we are usually wrong about our beloveds in the first throes of romance, when they are mainly just a blank screen for the projection of our own desires. Clarkson and McCall related how one of Trudeau's old schoolmates came to visit him before he had declared his candidacy for the Liberal leadership and warned him that he was far too shy to be a political leader. *Shy* was not a word that the general public would have associated with Trudeau, then or afterwards, but it was one often used by the people closest to him. He had that way of projecting his opposite, though also of pulling us up short with the unexpected, until it was impossible to say what was projection and what was real.

And yet, however mistaken we were in him, however unrealistic in our expectations, he still somehow managed to rise to every challenge. There would be other darlings who came after him who would enjoy their brief moments of deification—John Turner, Kim Campbell, Paul Martin Jr.—yet none would quite reach Trudeau's height and all would fall more precipitously. For a happenstance prime minister he was amazingly suited to his job: he had studied federalism and constitutional law; he had a solid grounding in economics; he knew the world. Above all he had an unfailing knack for being in the right place at the right moment, and for flourishing there when lesser men would have foundered.

With typical bravado, Trudeau had called for his first federal election to fall on the day after Quebec's annual airing of nationalist sentiment, the festival of Saint-Jean-Baptiste. At the invitation of mayor Jean Drapeau, Trudeau, on the day of the festival, had joined a host of other dignitaries on the reviewing stand of Montreal's Hôtel de Ville to watch as the parade filed by. There had been threats of violence if Trudeau showed up, and the police were out in force, but Trudeau himself sat front and centre on the reviewing stand, leaning out like a sports fan enjoying himself at a ball game.

Suddenly a hail of rocks and bottles rained down on the stand from protesters across the street. There was a flurry of movement as the gathered dignitaries and their spouses scrambled to get clear, but Trudeau kept his place. A second volley hit the stand and this time Trudeau's security men took hold of him to pull him away. He waved them off angrily and resumed his seat.

A cheer went up from the crowd.

The commentator for Radio Canada, which was televising the event, was unable to hide a note of awe.

"Monsieur Trudeau insiste il veut demeurer sur place."

Mask or no mask, this was not the sort of moment you could fake. Rather, before you could think, your character was revealed: you were the sort who fled, or you were the sort who stayed put. The next day, as people went to the polls, the image of Trudeau sticking defiantly to his place played on every TV screen in the country.

Once again, when the challenge came he was equal to it, as if he had been training for it all his life. In a sense, he had.

Whether he'd got there by choice or by chance, whether he'd been urged there or had led others to urge him, when he came to the sword he had what it took to pull it free.

CHAPTER THREE

Against the Current

The enduring image of Trudeau during his life, one he often encouraged, was that of someone who from a young age always chafed at conformity. His classmates took the side of the French, so he took the side the English; they spoke street Québécois, *joual*, so he made a point of speaking the French of Paris. In this way, Trudeau forged himself into the firebrand the country came to see him as when he was prime minister.

We now know that this image of Trudeau as someone who had sprung out of the womb a rebel and an original was largely a construction. Trudeau himself more or less admitted as much late in life in the introduction to a 1996 collection of his writings, *Against the Current,* where he remembered that in his early years he was "more inclined to do and say the conventional thing" than to question what he was taught. Though he'd grown more rebellious by his teens, "the real sea change came" when he returned to Quebec after graduate studies abroad and found that his province "had become a citadel of orthodoxy with a state-of-siege mentality. To remain a free man in Quebec, one had to go against the current of ideas and institutions."

This admission by Trudeau really goes to the heart of his political formation, even if it can't quite be taken at face value: he was the one who had changed much more than his province had, alive now to unpleasant aspects of his home culture to which he had been blind before his experience of the wider world. In many ways this more mature Trudeau, for all the sense people would later have of him as someone who had never wavered from certain core beliefs, came to hold views that were the polar opposites of those he had held as a youth. It would be hard to understand Trudeau's later political trajectory without understanding this crucial transitional period in his life and the demons he had had to wrestle with before he had got through it.

"MY CHILDHOOD having been a happy one," Trudeau wrote, "I felt no need for 'le doute méthodique.'" Happy, on the whole, his childhood may have been, but perhaps not quite in the generic way of Tolstoy's happy families. Trudeau's family stood out: a francophone father and anglophone mother, in an era when a kind of apartheid still reigned in Quebec between English and French; an increasing level of wealth that came not from some seigneurial past or from any of the traditional routes to respectability available to French Canadians—through the professions, mainly, particularly law—but through an entrepreneurial cunning that was entirely anomalous in French-Canadian society of the time.

If there was a true original in the Trudeau family, it was not Pierre but his father, Charles. Charles had indeed trained in the law but quickly grew bored with it and turned his mind to other pursuits. Correctly predicting the great future that lay ahead for the motor car, he started the Automobile Owners' Association, a sort of loyalty program that for a small membership fee offered discounted gas and repairs at Charlie's growing string of service stations. In 1932, by which time he had thirty stations and fifteen thousand members, he sold the business to Imperial Oil for $1.2 million. Then he took the money and made such clever investments—in mining, mostly, but also in an amusement park and the Montreal Royals baseball team—that in the very heart of the Depression he quickly managed to turn a small fortune into a much larger one.

Whatever hardships, then, Pierre may have endured while his father was establishing himself, by the time he was thirteen the family finances were such that money would not be a concern for him for the rest of his life. By then Charlie Trudeau, a hard-living bon vivant who dominated any room he was in and was forever holding late-night gatherings and jetting off to parts unknown, had apparently taken on a godlike status for the young Pierre, having managed by sheer force of will to pull the family up from the common lot into the upper crusts of Quebec society. Trudeau's take on his father in later life was usually as this exalted figure, slightly distant and unknowable, but all the more godlike for that. Yet the sheer energy of the man must have put a fright in him. It was Charlie's irritation at his son's frail, sensitive nature as a young boy that had started Trudeau on the path of the athleticism he was constantly parading in later life. In home movies of the time, Pierre was always mugging for the camera or engaging in antics that foreshadowed the ways his own sons would one day behave around him in an effort to get his attention. In any event, Charlie, in between his late nights and his business trips, set high standards for Pierre, and Pierre, whether in worship or terror, always did whatever it took to live up to them. Though by nature almost his father's opposite—retiring where his father was the consummate extrovert and tending toward the refined where his father tended toward the crude—much of what he became could be seen as a kind of offering to him, a re-channelling of his father's irrepressible energy and will through his own, very different character.

"My father was gregarious, outgoing, expansive," he told Gale Zoë Garnett years later. "I am not. Never have been. I am a solitaire, really. When I do something big and playful, like that pirouette behind the Queen, I am, I believe, pretending to be my father."

Just a few short years after he made the family rich, Charlie, never one to slow his pace for the sake of his health, fell dead from a heart attack. He was in Florida for the Royals' spring training when he came down with pneumonia. Pierre's mother and sister went to tend to him, though the next news Pierre and his brother Tip had in Montreal was of their father's death. Fifteen at the time, Trudeau said afterwards, "His death truly felt like the end of the world." His other reaction, however, was to think that "all of a sudden, I was more or less the head of a family; with him gone, it seemed to me that I had to take over." It might be simplistic to read an Oedipal wish-fulfillment in this thought, though over the next years—when he wasn't off at Harvard or the Sorbonne or chasing revolutions—Trudeau would come to fulfill this role as the family's head mainly with regard to his relationship with his mother, Grace. When Charlie died, Grace came out of the shadows to become a dominating presence not only in the family but on the Montreal social scene, and the man who was invariably on her arm when she was out and about was her son Pierre, who kept rooms in the family home into his forties and didn't marry until his mother had passed into senility.

Clarkson and McCall, in their own speculation about the impact of Charlie's death on Pierre, extensively mined exactly this Freudian vein, seeing the sudden disappearance of "the most powerful presence" in Trudeau's life as the source of a "psychic imbalance" Trudeau could never get beyond. "The day would never come … when paternal dominance would be replaced by the father's acknowledgement of the son's achievements as a grown man." Later biographers have been skeptical of this analysis, taking Trudeau's reaction to his father's death somewhat more at face value, as the normal grieving of an adolescent at the loss of a beloved parent. But whatever twist one gives it, the death would surely have marked Trudeau profoundly, and likely in ways which neither his own comments on it nor the comments of those around him would have plumbed the depths of. Clearly it was something that hung over Trudeau all his life—forty years later the memory of it could still bring tears to his eyes—not least for the fact that the tremendous freedom he enjoyed throughout his life to do as he wished rested largely on the fortune that Charlie had almost literally killed himself to amass.

In the short term, at least, the death may have brought some feeling of liberation along with the trauma. Suddenly Trudeau was free of this larger-than-life figure he had been trying to please all his childhood. This was the period in which a so-called anti-authoritarian streak began to come out in Trudeau at school, the elite Jesuit *lycée* Jean-de-Brébeuf, which had opened its doors in Montreal just a few years earlier. The streak manifested itself, however, mainly in a prankishness that seemed more calculated to call attention to Trudeau than to overthrow the established order. Even in the year of his father's death, Trudeau managed to win awards and keep up his high academic standing. The evidence, in fact, suggests that far from becoming a maverick in these years, Trudeau, like most adolescents, was instead doing everything he could to be accepted and to fit in, tailoring himself to his differing environments in a way that went very much with the current rather than against it.

At home, where the reign of Grace had now replaced the reign of Charles, the atmosphere had grown increasingly English and refined. Gone were the late nights, the physicality, the coarse language and jokes. "When my father was around, there was a great deal of effusiveness and laughter and kissing and hugging," he told biographer George Radwanski. "But after he died, it was a little bit more the

English mores which took over, and we used to even joke about, or laugh at, some of our cousins or neighbours or friends—French Canadians—who'd always be very effusive within the family and towards their mothers and so on."

But while he was becoming increasingly English at home, at school, in an almost Zelig-like compartmentalization, he was becoming increasingly French. There, his father's death seemed to have had the effect of leading him to seek out father figures among his Jesuit teachers, men whose difference from his father prompts the question whether Trudeau was trying to fill a lack or rather explore a new freedom. Some of these teachers were to exercise an enormous influence over him, in ways that were not generally known until Trudeau biographer John English and former *Cité libre* editors Max and Monique Nemni were granted access to Trudeau's archive after his death. What these researchers found was a portrait of Trudeau's formation substantially at odds with the standard, accepted version during his life.

In their groundbreaking book *Young Trudeau: 1919–1944,* Max and Monique Nemni use materials from the Trudeau archive to show how, far from learning at Brébeuf, as one of his teachers was to claim, the values of "federalism, democracy, and pluralism" that would become the bedrock of Trudeau's beliefs in later years, he was instead initiated into a brand of reactionary nationalism very much at odds with these values but quite common in Quebec in the years preceding the Second World War. Trudeau was in the habit of keeping thorough records, even going so far as to save drafts of his letters, and his archive contains a treasure trove of notebooks and journals and papers of every sort. Using these, the Nemnis have shown that the Trudeau who emerged from Brébeuf was one who subscribed not only to the widespread anti-Semitism of the day but to the church's disdain for democracy.

In Quebec, the church's preferred model of governance in that period was a so-called corporatist one, in which the state acted as a sort of benevolent parent, governing citizens who couldn't be trusted to govern themselves. This was the very model that lay behind the fascist dictatorships then gaining ascendancy in Europe. The church's ultimate goal in Quebec was an independent state that functioned as a kind of theocracy, Catholic and ethnically pure. In an essay Trudeau wrote at Brébeuf about his hopes for the future, he imagined just such a prospect. After establishing himself as an international war hero, he would return home "around the year 1976" just in time to lead the charge in the establishment of an independent Quebec that was "Catholic and *canadien*."

Canadien, in Quebec, was always a term that referred not to Canadians as a whole but only to the "real" Canadians, the descendants of the pre-Conquest French *habitants.* Putting aside the unintentional irony of Trudeau's reference to 1976—the year René Lévesque's Parti Québécois would come to power—the swashbuckling tone of the essay was decidedly tongue-in-cheek. But this was not satire: however much Trudeau might have been indulging in a flight of fancy, he was doing so within terms that would not only have been accepted at Brébeuf but encouraged. The point comes through more starkly in a play the Nemnis quote that Trudeau wrote for the college's tenth-anniversary celebrations. Originally titled *On est Canadiens français ou on ne l'est pas,* a popular nationalist saying of the day, but then changed to *Dupés,* "duped," the play's apparent message was that Jewish merchants were stealing the livelihoods of French Canadians. The idea echoed a buy-from-our-own campaign being championed at the time by the outspoken cleric and nationalist leader Abbé Lionel Groulx.

If Trudeau was rebelling against anything at this age, it certainly wasn't the narrow-minded nationalism that later made Quebec seem "a citadel of orthodoxy" to him. Yet his writings of the time were full of the *language* of rebellion. In *Dupés,* a character named Ditreau, who claims a diploma in "commercial psychology," advises the French-Canadian tailor Couture to pretend to be a Jew to improve his business. French Canadians, Ditreau says, prefer to buy from Jews, "firstly because they don't want to enrich one of their own and then because they believe they will get a better price." Couture goes along at first, then rebels. "Now it's my turn to teach a lesson: the *Canadien* people is a sleeping lion. It will soon awaken." Perhaps this was exactly the appeal of nationalism to someone of Trudeau's disposition, that it allowed all the rhetoric of rebellion without costing him the approval of his superiors. One almost senses even in *Dupés,* which had the same tongue-in-cheek tone as his essay on his hopes for the future, that the actual content was just an excuse for indulging a certain irreverence. Ditreau—his name was an obvious play on "Trudeau," who in fact played him in the production—can't help but strike us now as offensive, but there is also a mischievousness to him that cuts in both directions.

Trudeau noted on his copy of the script that the play was presented "before parents and students with great success." Success seems to have been the point for him. A few days earlier he had taken it very hard when he had lost a student election to his friend and great rival at Brébeuf, Jean de Grandpré, the same man who would later come to advise him not to run for the Liberal leadership. By now, as if to reconcile the double life he had begun to lead, Pierre had taken to including his matronymic, Elliott, as part of his name, but he had cause to wonder if it had cost him the election. In *Citizen of the World*, John English describes how Trudeau learned of an accusation made behind his back that he was "mediocre, Americanized, and Anglicized, in short, I would betray my race." For Trudeau the accusation was "a profound shock." "I would never betray the French Canadians," he wrote in his journal. But he was also determined to retain his own Englishness, which he thought— not entirely correctly, it seems—helped give him the strength to resist simply following "the popular spirit." "I am proud of my English blood, which comes from my mother. At least it tempers my boiling French blood. It leaves me calmer and more insightful and perspicacious."

This kind of reflection on a dual heritage is very familiar to the children of immigrants, who grow up fighting dual claims in almost every arena. What is surprising with Trudeau is how seldom the issue seems to have come up for open discussion, not only in his youth but also in his later political life. Even though his doubleness formed an important part of his public image, there always seemed a taboo around any actual allusion to it. One infamous breaking of this taboo was René Lévesque's snide and ill-considered reference to Trudeau's "Elliott" side just days before the 1980 referendum, in much the same terms as the anonymous accusation levelled at Trudeau back at Brébeuf. This time, Trudeau was able to give as good he got, in a rousing speech at Paul Sauvé Arena that cost Lévesque the high ground and may have cost him the referendum. Back at Brébeuf, however, Trudeau, for all his self-reflection, showed little understanding of the essentially irreconcilable conflict between his own Englishness and his growing allegiance to an anti-English ethnic nationalism.

As a young man, in an apparent compromise, Trudeau came to refer to his mother not as English but as Scottish. At Brébeuf, however, what may have helped him to abide his contradictions was that his mother had inherited French blood from her own mother, along with an ardent Catholicism that was always to remain a strong point of contact between her and her son. When Trudeau was at home, he never missed a Mass with his mother, and their shared faith may have served as a sort of bridge for him, a point of reconciliation between the English world of home and French one of Brébeuf, where he attended Mass as often as three times a day. Trudeau, for all his aura of rationalism and secularism, was to remain a staunch Catholic the rest of his life, faltering briefly in his faith, according to friends, only at the time of the death of his son Michel. One reason, perhaps, that his Catholicism remained so central to him was because of this unifying role it had had for him as an adolescent, holding together his disparate selves.

TRUDEAU EMERGED from Collège Jean-de-Brébeuf steeped in views that were fairly typical for his time and place and social class. Trudeau himself, however, was hardly typical. At Brébeuf he had been, as he would later be, a star. That quality would perhaps remain the real constant in his life, his ability to excel, to shine in the right ways and at the right moment. The skill seemed less the result of some natural flair than of an iron discipline, one that went back to the pains he had taken to please his father but that had been honed to a razor edge by the Jesuits at Brébeuf. He had mastered every subject there, and in his final year beat even his rival Jean de Grandpré to stand first in the school; he had read extensively, always beyond the required texts, and had written commentaries on everything he had read. He had been the captain of the hockey team; he had skied, played lacrosse, swum, boxed, and sailed. He had had his debates and his plays, his student politics and his student paper, had played piano and gone to the symphony. Among a group of already exceptional students, he had been more exceptional, for which he had been rewarded with prizes—often, to his pleasure, in cash—and with praise.

When he emerged from this cocoon of adulation and familiarity, however, schooled in an ideology designed to prepare him to take his place in the French-Canadian elite, he promptly attempted to flee his French self and indulge his English one, applying for a Rhodes Scholarship to study at Oxford. Until then he had expressed his hopes for the future mainly in the vague, lofty terms adolescents are given to. "I would like so much to be a great politician and to guide my nation," he had written in his journal in 1938, though he had also flirted with the idea of joining the priesthood. In his Rhodes application, however, he stated quite unequivocally that he planned to pursue a career in politics. "For some years now," he wrote, "I have sought out activities that prepare one most immediately for public life," among which he included his diction lessons, his acting, and his singing lessons. Whether Trudeau, in the time-honoured manner of application-fillers, was merely trying to suggest some pattern to what might otherwise seem a hopeless hodgepodge, the idea of politics had at least crossed his mind by now, even if in his play, *Dupés;* Trudeau's character Ditreau had been rejected by his beloved for being that vilest of things, a politician.

For once, Trudeau failed to get the prize. The Rhodes, despite his impressive credentials and glowing references, went to another candidate. Unexpectedly, Trudeau found himself at loose ends, and as a fallback began to study law at the Université de Montréal. In the meantime, the Second World War had broken out. In his memoirs, Trudeau gave the impression that he paid as little attention to the war as he could get away with. "[T]he instinct that made me go against prevailing opinion caused me to affect a certain air of indifference. So there was a war? Tough. It wouldn't stop me from concentrating on my studies so long as that was possible."

Again, Trudeau may have overplayed in hindsight his resistance to "prevailing opinion," not to mention his interest in his studies. His studies, in fact, bored him. Though he performed with his usual brilliance, graduating, in 1943, once more at the top of his class, he often spoke dismissively of law school at the time, and never with any of the excitement with which he spoke of his days at Brébeuf. The one lasting legacy of his years there, perhaps, was that it was where he first came across a man who would later prove a great influence on him, the law professor, constitutional expert and civil libertarian, F.R. Scott, who spoke at the university in 1943 on the question of conscription. At the time, though, Trudeau was apparently just as taken with an extracurricular lecture by Abbé Lionel Groulx, who, despite being a man of the cloth, spoke on the conditions under which armed insurrection could be justified, using the Lower Canada Rebellion of 1837–38 as his example.

Most of Trudeau's time at law school, however, was taken up not with his studies but with exactly the sorts of issues which he later claimed to have had little involvement in. If in his desire to go to England—though only as a scholar; he'd shown no interest in going as a soldier—he had at some level been expressing a wish to escape the narrowness of Quebec nationalist culture, now that he was stuck in it he very much continued to play his part. In his memoirs, he shrugged off a speech he gave at an anti-conscription rally as a momentary effort that had less to do with the war than with the affront to democracy shown by the federal government's reversal on conscription. In reality, however, Trudeau's speech was the culmination of many weeks of involvement in a federal by-election on behalf of the anti-conscription candidate Jean Drapeau. The speech itself, given at a rally in the campaign's final days, made such an impression that *Le Devoir* quoted great portions of it. Speaking of the hysteria he claimed the government was stirring up of an imminent German invasion, Trudeau said he "feared the peaceful invasion of immigrants"—often a code word for Jews—"more than the armed invasion of the enemy." While in the past, he went on, the French Canadians had had to fight against the Iroquois, "today it is against other savages" they had to fight, namely the Mackenzie King Liberals in Ottawa.

All of this went far beyond the innocent defence of democratic principles into the truly hateful. It was demagoguery; it was, in this man who would later be known by the motto "Reason over passion," an appeal to the basest impulses. At twenty-three, Trudeau was still clearly of his times rather than above them. As at Brébeuf, he was still attracted to the rhetoric of revolution, but as then, he took care to apply it in a way more likely to earn him accolades than billy clubs.

The other holdover from Brébeuf, however, was Trudeau's telltale playfulness. The speech was full of inside jokes and puns, playing throughout on the name Drapeau, or flag, and that of Drapeau's rival, La Flèche, or arrow. It ended with the line "Enough of *cataplasmes* [bandages], bring on the cataclysms," exactly the sort of clever formulation the young Trudeau revelled in, at once rousing and comic. As odious as the speech was, then, it bore the trace of the same doubleness as his play, *Dupés,* a tone of mockery whose target remained unclear. Self-mockery, perhaps, but also a kind of subconscious escape clause, as if, in a pinch, one could claim to others, or to oneself, not to have been speaking seriously. The stakes were higher now than at Brébeuf—this was the real world, with real consequences—but Trudeau still seemed to be hiding behind the same mask, half-denying even as he affirmed. Perhaps that was what lay behind his later claim that he hadn't involved himself much in politics during the war: the sense that he hadn't, really, not in some essential part of himself, had merely been playing a role. In one of his pranks during the war years, he and a friend dressed up in old Prussian uniforms and toured the countryside on their Harleys calling on friends and frightening passersby, who perhaps thought that the Huns had truly arrived at their shores.

If he was playing a role, however, he seemed prepared to take it to extremes. At Brébeuf, Trudeau had come under the influence of one of the more politicized teachers, Father Rodolphe Dubé, better known by his pen name, François Hertel. In 1939 Hertel had published *Le beau risque,* a nationalist coming-of-age tale in which the young Pierre Martel turns away from the Anglicized and Americanized values of his father toward a renewed Catholicism and devotion to his *patrie.* Martel's life so clearly paralleled Trudeau's that Hertel had surely used him as a model, though Trudeau, who reviewed the book in his journal, gave no indication of recognizing the resemblances.

After leaving Brébeuf, Trudeau kept up contact with Hertel, who was a frequent guest at the Trudeau home. In *Young Trudeau,* the Nemnis have made a convincing case that Trudeau was involved with Hertel and several of his old Brébeuf schoolmates in a secret society called "*les X*" or "L.X.," also referred to as *les Frères chasseurs.* The society's mission was the establishment of an independent Quebec organized on Catholic and corporatist—in other words, fascist—principles. Through the summer of 1942, Trudeau and his friend Jean-Baptiste Boulanger worked on what they called the "Plan," using writers like Trudeau's beloved Plato to direct them, but also the anti-Semitic and anti-democratic Charles Maurras, a strong supporter of Marshall Pétain's Vichy government. After several drafts they came up with a manifesto that summarized their aim as a "national revolution," which they saw as "a permanent struggle aimed at the human excellence of the community." The country to emerge from this revolution, the manifesto concluded, would be "Catholic, French and Laurentian" and would express itself "in a State that is at the same time authoritarian and the guardian of freedoms."

The Nemnis were able to track later references to the society by some of its former members. Hertel, for instance, admitted Trudeau's involvement in it to *La Presse* in 1977, even ascribing its formation to Trudeau. The playwright and actor Jean-Louis Roux, meanwhile, wrote about the society in his memoirs, recalling a document that was passed around explaining how the city's police and fire stations would be captured and its radio stations occupied when the day of action came. Roux later paid heavily for his own antics during the war, losing an appointment as Quebec's lieutenant-governor when it became known he had worn a swastika as a part of anti-conscription protest. But Trudeau, for some reason, was spared, even though many of the details about his wartime activities would have been readily available to journalists during his lifetime.

On the eventual fate of *les X*, the Nemnis have been unable to offer much direction. The paper trail ends in 1943; the society may have gone on working for years in deepest secrecy or may simply have collapsed from its own irrelevance. "Parfaitement loufoque," Roux said of the enterprise, perfectly nutty, and it had enough of the same suspicious tone of highhanded irreverence of many of Trudeau's earlier projects for one to wonder how seriously its own members took it. At the end of the manifesto for the group that Trudeau and Boulanger had written up, they had tacked the line "God approves." Another document that outlined methods for dealing with traitors included "temporary kidnapping" among its suggestions. Roux, who announced he was quitting the group when it gave him the ludicrous task of recruiting to it the secretary general of the Université de Montréal, Édouard Montpetit, was made to believe that severe repercussions awaited those who tried to drop out. "The days, the weeks, the months went by," Roux recalled later. "Nothing occurred. I'm still waiting."

We may never really know if the young man whose rebelliousness at Brébeuf had seldom risen above the level of throwing snowballs was truly plotting a fascist coup—with what would have had to have been a nearly psychotic level of delusion—or if the whole project was merely an intellectual exercise to relieve the boredom of law school or confound his future biographers. This last possibility is a real one. In a commentary he wrote at Brébeuf on Pascal's *Pensées* that is reproduced by the Nemnis, the young Trudeau reflected at length, with eerie foresight, on his future biographers. After admitting that pride—the fear he might later look ridiculous—often prevented him from putting down his true thoughts, he then admitted to the greater pride beyond this fear, namely the assumption "that some day biographers will delve into all that we have written down to follow therein the development of our thinking." He went on in that vein, trying to find the way around a self-consciousness that only became more tortuous and inescapable the more he explored it. "Pascal, writing down his thoughts," he concluded, "was more assured of surviving than I am (more assured because of his previous success, but not more convinced! Such is my assurance.) (I have this assurance because I'm role playing, and not so much because it's definitely within me.)"

By the end of the passage we feel as if we are in a house of mirrors, with no basis anymore for ascertaining which image is the true one. Trudeau, in a tone at once whimsical and troubled, gave us a window here onto a complexity of character that was both a sort of freedom and a sort of prison, that multiplied his possible selves but left him caught up in a self-consciousness that then gave the lie to each of them. "If you want to know my thoughts," Trudeau started his journal of 1938, "read between the lines!" The self-consciousness, the presumed audience, was always there, making every statement somehow doubly suspect. It would be a risk to take at face value the writings of a young man in whom self-revelation and self-concealment were so interwoven.

John English notes in *Citizen of the World* that radical groups like *les X* were quite common in Quebec during the war. Gérard Pelletier recalled in his memoirs that Jean

Marchand, too, "had been recruited into one of the innumerable leagues that existed at the time (each one with twelve or fifteen members), all of which wanted to overthrow the government and put an end to democracy. That was the spirit of the age." That same spirit would return some years later in the FLQ, only this time with real bombs and with real kidnappings. Trudeau by then would find himself on a very different side of the question, though some of the parallels between the two periods may provide insight into the younger Trudeau. There was something reminiscent of the young Pierre Trudeau in Hubert Aquin, for instance, the author, intellectual, and would-be felquiste who served time in a psychiatric hospital after announcing he was going underground to become a terrorist. In Aquin's semi-autobiographical novel *Prochain épisode,* a narrator imprisoned for an unnamed revolutionary crime recounts a sort of spy story set around Lake Geneva that is a complex allegory of Quebec's oppression and of the narrator's, and Aquin's, own experience. In its self-consciousness and reflexivity, where reality and fantasy become difficult to separate, the book recalls the writings of the young Trudeau, refusing ever to settle squarely on a clear self-characterization or on a single plan of action or point of view. Aquin was arrested after he declared his terrorist intentions but was never convicted of any crime, and his life reads much less like that of a revolutionary than that of a tortured intellectual who was unable to escape the straitjacket of his cultural identity or the frustration of his own inaction. After discussing suicide with the people around him for many years, in a running dialogue that almost became a kind of farce, he finally shot himself outside a Catholic girls' school in Montreal.

Aquin was perhaps the extreme end of the kind of circular self-consciousness the young Trudeau manifested, one that intellectuals in the hothouse culture of Quebec would have been particularly prone to whenever the calls of nationalism and collective loyalty made it difficult to indulge the usual ambiguities and doubts of an intelligent mind. The portrait of Trudeau that emerges from the war years is of someone living a divided identity, throwing himself full force into a lunatic revolutionary movement as if to prove he would never be the one to betray his race, as his anonymous accuser at Brébeuf had suggested, yet still winning his accolades at school, and still living out his Englishness at home.

Over the years there would be many casualties among Quebec nationalists of men who, like Aquin, were never able to reconcile the contradictions between collective and self. It may have been the church, again, that helped save Trudeau. His extracurricular readings of the time included not only reactionaries like Charles Maurras and André Tardieu—and his commentaries on these were disturbingly uncritical—but also Catholic writers like Pascal and François Mauriac and Henri Bergson, who were somewhat more in the mainstream of Western thought. From them he would draw the ideas that became the basis both for his later "personalist" approach to his faith and for the values that would come to define his view of the individual and of human rights. The faith that had bound him to a regressive nationalism would also be his way free of it. In the 1950s, his personalism would make him one of the leading critics in Quebec of a church hierarchy whose paternalism and authoritarianism he had sought to glorify during the war.

At Brébeuf, where Trudeau valued his religion classes above all others, he jotted down these notes inspired by a teacher, Father Lamarche, for whom he had had a tremendous respect. "See the truth wherever it is to be found. If one is not strong enough to act accordingly, that is too bad. But one should at least be loyal enough to recognize that what is true is true." These words sound like the Trudeau we would all eventually come to know. But if something in him during his war years in Quebec saw through to the truth, he was not "strong enough to act accordingly." He went with the current. When the atrocities in Europe began to be widely known he dismissed them as propaganda, as many Quebecers did, writing a vicious parody of Mackenzie King's renewed call to arms for the university paper. Meanwhile he attended rallies that turned into anti-Semitic riots. He also staged a play in which Adam Dollard des Ormeaux, killed by the Iroquois in the 1600s, stood for the embattled French Canadians and the Iroquois, as in his anti-conscription speech, stood for the savage English (although Trudeau, always layering in his ambiguities, played an Iroquois in the actual production). In one of his more bizarre escapades, related by the Nemnis in *Young Trudeau,* he turned a debate on gallantry into an elaborate anti-British protest, lacing his comments with double meanings and planting his fellow *Frères chasseurs* in the audience to help further the spectacle. In the final moments, one of Trudeau's plants pretended to heckle him and Trudeau pulled out a gun loaded with blanks and fired it at him. He then turned his back to the audience and made a gesture of being hanged, ending by pointing to his backside and suggesting a Union Jack be planted there.

We may recognize the later Trudeau in the style of these antics but not so much in their intent. In 2004 the CBC released a peculiar drama called *Maverick in the Making,* in which the young Trudeau was depicted as many of us would have imagined him in these years: attending anti-Franco meetings, getting beaten up by the Montreal fascists, fighting the church establishment at every turn. Many of these scenes have so much the ring of truth that one has to keep reminding oneself that they are pure fabrication. At one point Pierre goes to confession, and just before launching into a diatribe against church authority he asks the priest if it is possible that the war against the Nazis is a just one. But there is little evidence that this question ever occurred to the real Trudeau at the time.

Trudeau's flurry of public actions ended abruptly when he graduated from law school in 1943, as did his subversive activities with *les X* and a period of intense reading and writing and publication. For reasons that aren't entirely clear, he had also grown suddenly bitter and disillusioned. In a jotting that was never published he wrote, "If the ordinary people truly realized what sort it was they were relying on to ensure salvation … they would not wait another day before giving up altogether." He had been disappointed by his own co-conspirators, or perhaps by the whole future elite of Quebec with whom he had just spent three years at law school, and whom he accused of being utterly "two-faced" and lacking in character.

Obviously "two-faced," in Trudeau's lexicon, was much more heinous than many-faced, as he was. Yet his bitterness seemed genuine: he had seen past some scrim, had seen the divide between talk and action. He himself, despite a legitimate claim to divided loyalties, had been willing to give over the whole of his energies to the call of the collectivity. He may have found that others, for all their talk, were not quite so ready to rise to the challenge.

A YEAR OF ARTICLING was enough for Trudeau to grow bored, as his father had, with the practice of law. "[T]hat's the problem when you have an office," he told George Radwanski. "People come to you with their problems." Then, in 1944, he finally received permission from Canadian authorities, denied the previous year on account of the war, to leave the country to study in the United States. The next years would prove crucial. As John English shows in *Citizen of the World,* through Trudeau's correspondence and other writings of this period, the man who left Quebec feeling intellectually bankrupt and hollowed out would return to it five years later with an outlook that was much changed from that of his youth, and that would come to define him for the rest of his life.

Trudeau had chosen to go to Harvard, to study "Political Economy and Government." In his memoirs, he said he had been torn "between law, psychology, sociology, and political science." After consulting many people, including the great Quebec intellectual and political leader Henri Bourassa, by then in his seventies, Trudeau finally took the advice of André Laurendeau, at the time a Quebec MNA, who pointed out to him that Quebec was sadly lacking in economists. In his Harvard application, however, Trudeau stayed true to the hope he had expressed when he had applied for a Rhodes Scholarship to follow a career in politics. "I need not hide my conviction that Canada is decidedly lacking in statesmen. We French-Canadians in particular have too few political thinkers to lead us, and the sight of such splendid people going to ruin appalls me."

It did not take Trudeau long to realize how blinkered his life in Quebec had been over the previous few years. In his memoirs, he recalled that in the "super-informed environment" of Harvard, he began to grasp, for the first time, the "true dimensions" of the war. Harvard had on faculty several professors who had fled the Nazis, including Hitler's predecessor as chancellor, Heinrich Brüning. "I realized then that I had, as it were, missed one of the major events of the century in which I was living."

A great deal seemed to go unstated in this recollection. He ended it thus: "Did I feel any regret? No. I have always regarded regret as a useless emotion." But as the war was ending in 1945, he wrote to the girlfriend he had left behind in Montreal expressing exactly that, regret, seeming mortified at the mindset that had allowed him to remain caught up his own partisan pursuits while unimaginable horrors were occurring across the sea. His laments had the quality of a *cri di cœur*—understandably so, given that the "true dimensions" of the war had been well enough known for some time by then, and he had chosen to discount them. As much as he later downplayed this moment of revelation, it was likely determinative for him in setting the future course of his thinking.

Trudeau's notes from the time show he had been reading up on Fascism and National Socialism and understanding how narrow and unreflective his own political thinking had been. Commenting on one of his readings he noted that "democracy is not synonymous with capitalistic exploitation," with the tone of someone who had just emerged from a pampered dictatorship to discover that the wider world was not the den of iniquity he had been led to believe.

Trudeau mentioned that Heinrich Brüning, a Catholic, had fled the Nazis for Harvard, but he didn't mention any Jews who had found refuge from the Nazis there, probably because none had. Despite the massive influx of Jewish intellectuals into the United States before and during the war,

Harvard, in addition to a tacit quota on Jewish students, maintained a virtual moratorium on the hiring of Jewish faculty well into the 1940s. This "super-informed environment" was not exactly super-enlightened. Trudeau, however, an outsider now, keeping to his room in the graduate residence much of the time despite the "Citizen of the World" tag pinned to his door, and making few friends, might have grown more sensitive to other outsiders. A friend he did make, in fact, was fellow graduate student Louis Hartz, who became a sort of mentor. He was one of the few Jews who had managed to slip in under the quota and would later go on to become a full professor at Harvard and one of its most influential political scientists.

Though Trudeau later spoke enthusiastically about his time at Harvard, his letters of the time, quoted at length by John English, show he was not very happy there. From having been the centre of attention he was suddenly a provincial; and everything he had learned and thought, his entire formation, must suddenly have seemed a bill of goods. Outside the conformist atmosphere of Quebec, where it had been possible to indulge his rebelliousness simply by subscribing to the views of his superiors, he was discovering ways of making sense of the world that he had never considered. Much of his later intransigence toward Quebec nationalists likely went back to this time, when the scales fell from his eyes and he realized how blinded he had been by his own nationalism.

Even so, he allowed himself to ease toward a new understanding only by a kind of "*étapisme,*" not so much renouncing old views as reasoning toward new ones, as if to save himself the shock of complete reversal. One part of his past education he was happy to leave behind, however, was his time at law school: he now had confirmed for him what he had suspected all along, that much of what he had been taught there was beside the point. It was at Harvard that he came to understand the law not as a dull collection of jots and tittles but, as he would later tell Peter Newman when he became justice minister, as a structure for "planning for the society of tomorrow," the very warp and woof of what held a society together. He also received a solid grounding in economics at Harvard, one of the reasons, after all, he had chosen to go there. He later tended to downplay his understanding of economics, always stressing his cultured side over his political one, but at Harvard he studied with people like the pre-eminent post-Keynesian economist John Kenneth Galbraith and the eventual Nobel laureate Wassily Leontief. It was at Harvard that he was first exposed to the Keynesian theories of interventionism that would guide his own years in office. But there were also many opponents of Keynes at Harvard who left their mark. In *Citizen of the World,* John English makes the argument that what many people later took as a lack of rigour in Trudeau's economic thinking was really the understanding he took from the divergent views he was exposed to at Harvard that "economic judgements were not the product of a science but more often the result of special interests." What in Trudeau the politician came across as indifference to economics, then, may more properly have been distrust of it.

In later years Trudeau would give the impression that Harvard had merely confirmed him on a path he had already been on. The evidence, however, suggests that it was exactly at Harvard that the ideas that later defined him first took root. His writings of the time show that what he took from Harvard was not simple theory but a growing understanding of the complex ways in which societies function and of how their various aspects—their laws, their economies, their political systems—interconnect. From someone who had had a suspicion of liberalism and democracy and capitalism bred into him from a young age, he was becoming a grudging convert. He was also starting to understand how pie-in-the-sky some of his youthful ideas had been. Back in Montreal, writing his manifestos for *les X,* he hadn't given much thought to how his Laurentian state would put food on the table.

In 1946 he earned his master's from Harvard and went on to Paris to do courses at the École libre des sciences politiques and the Sorbonne. His plan was to begin research for a doctorate on the relationship between Christianity and Communism, a topic that showed how far he had come in his thinking in his two years at Harvard. In Paris he ended up spending little time in class, however, and much more touring the cafés with old acquaintances from Quebec he had met up with there. These included Gérard Pelletier, whose close, lifelong friendship with Trudeau really dated to this time; Roger Rolland, who had been part of Trudeau's Prussian soldier prank; Jean-Louis Roux, who presumably was still awaiting his reprisals from *les X;* and his former Brébeuf mentor, François Hertel. In 1947 Hertel would be expelled from the Jesuits for his controversial views, and eventually his trenchant nationalism would result in a bitter split between him and Trudeau. But for now his presence brought Trudeau away from his Harvard liberalism and back to the question of religion.

It was during his time in Paris that Trudeau came to embrace personalism, a philosophy that was to provide him another bridge between the values he had grown up with and the ones he was evolving toward. Founded by the French thinker Emmanuel Mounier, personalism was a sort of spiritualized existentialism, asserting the primacy of the individual and of free will but balancing these with the demands of social conscience and social responsibility. For Trudeau, the philosophy became—perhaps a bit conveniently—a means both of holding on to his past and of remaking it, transforming a Catholicism that in Quebec had consisted of a close-minded authoritarianism into one consonant with the principles of liberal democracy and individualism. Implicit in the philosophy was an almost Protestant notion of personal conscience that would later serve as a bulwark for Trudeau in his battles with the priest-based Catholicism of Quebec.

Another great influence on Trudeau at the time was the French philosopher and political thinker Jacques Maritain, a Catholic convert who advocated a philosophy he called integral humanism. Like personalism, it sought a way to reintroduce the spiritual element that had been lost in secular humanism. As one of the drafters of the Universal Declaration of Human Rights in 1947, Maritain was a key figure in establishing the notion of inalienable rights that would one day motivate Trudeau's own Charter. The Nemnis point out, however, that when Trudeau had read

Maritain in 1944 while still in Quebec, he had not been especially impressed, accusing him of hanging on "to a backward-looking democracy" and of being "right out of it" where practical issues were concerned.

From Paris, without having accomplished much in terms of his studies, Trudeau moved on after a year to the London School of Economics, abandoning his dissertation on Communism and Christianity to start a new doctoral program in political science. Friendless again, Trudeau found London a repeat of his experience at Harvard. For a "citizen of the world," he was not yet very adept at negotiating unfamiliar environments, and he found postwar London a tremendous letdown after Paris. At the LSE, however, he studied under the world-renowned leftist Harold Laski, who ended up having a tremendous influence on him. Trudeau had been drawn to the left during his time in Paris, where Communism had been very much in vogue and even the personalists leaned toward a kind of Christian socialism. Now Laski, a mythic presence at the LSE, drew him further. Laski had a towering intellect but was also a brilliant and beloved teacher—and someone who, like Trudeau, relished a good fight.

Laski was also a Jew. In his memoirs, Trudeau made frequent references to the wide range of humanity he encountered in his studies abroad, a situation that was "a complete change from the rather parochial climate" he had known growing up in Montreal. In all likelihood, the notion of multiculturalism Trudeau later came to espouse in Canada actually had its roots in these first real experiences outside the country. The Montreal of his childhood was hardly monocultural, yet he had lived it as such, where everyone who was other—the English, the immigrants, the Jews—was the enemy. Now the boundaries between "us" and "them" were dissolving; it was in this sense that he truly became a "citizen of the world." Now his friends were Jews; now his professor and mentor was. Canada didn't make him a pluralist; the world did, in these very personal bonds he developed—first in his studies and later in his travels—with people who had previously been entirely outside the realm of his experience.

According to John English, Laski, as one of the major thinkers in the British socialist movement, became a model for Trudeau of the "engaged intellectual." In Laski, Trudeau saw what he himself could be. Trudeau later said that it was in London that "everything I had learned until then of law, economics, political science, and political philosophy came together for me." Indeed, the titles of his courses with Laski read like a checklist for every tool Trudeau would later need in his political toolkit: "Democracy and the British

Constitution," "Liberalism," and "Revolution." Even Trudeau's understanding of federalism went back to Laski: the sharing of power in federal systems was one of Laski's major areas of interest.

Trudeau completed a year of studies at the LSE but, as at the Sorbonne, he obtained no degree, having by now abandoned the idea of a doctorate. Before returning home, however, he set himself one more "challenge," as he put it: he had decided to travel the world. Rather than sticking to the well-worn routes, however, he intended "to range more widely." To that end he would eschew the more comfortable means of travel he could well have afforded in favour of those "of Everyman," going on foot, by bus, by cargo boat, the better "to mix with local populations" and "learn their habits, their troubles, and their reactions."

Despite the slightly anthropological tone of his description of it, the trip proved to be as crucial, in its way, to Trudeau's later political career as his international studies would be. For one thing, much of the mystique that surrounded him, and in particular the sense of his having been a hippie *avant la lettre* that so appealed to young people, derived from this trip. But just as importantly, the trip humbled him. The stories that were told afterwards were the dramatic ones, the arrests and near-arrests, the wars and the revolutions. But in later years what always struck people who travelled with Trudeau was his tremendous humility as a traveller, his ability to immerse himself in a foreign culture without presuming to know better than his hosts. It was a humility, according to Trudeau's son Alexandre, that went back to this first trip.

Alexandre's foreword to a 2007 reissue of *Two Innocents in Red China*—an account by his father and Jacques Hébert of a trip they took together in 1960—talked about the importance of his father's earlier round-the-world trip, when for first time Trudeau stepped beyond the borders of the "well-established social values" he had been able to depend on until then.

> In the Canadian wilds, he had deliberately deprived himself of physical and even psychological shelter, but he had never had to deal with the near total absence of all moral shelter. In his great journey of 1949 he found himself on many occasions without the protection of the rule of law, in situations where he had to rely for survival not on his own wits or strength of limb, but on a force completely beyond his control: the kindness of strangers.

It was a very different Trudeau who would return to Quebec at the end of 1949 than the one who had left it in 1944. It was still not quite the Trudeau we would come to know of, or the Trudeau we would think we knew, but by now all the scaffolding was in place.

CHAPTER FOUR

Cité libre

Trudeau, at thirty, returned from overseas to be immersed almost at once in an event that truly marked his emergence as a public figure, the Asbestos Strike in Quebec's Eastern Townships. The strike was a turning point in the Quebec union movement, pitting the French-Canadian working class not only against the English bosses who ran the mines and the foreign bosses who owned them, but against the Quebec leader who allowed these bosses free rein, Maurice Duplessis. Duplessis, the founder of the ultra-conservative Union Nationale, would rule Quebec with near-dictatorial force until his death in 1959, in a reign that would come to be known as *la Grande noirceur,* the "Great Darkness."

It was through the strike that the future Three Wise Men first came together. Trudeau had hardly unpacked before Gérard Pelletier, who was covering the strike for *Le Devoir,* drove him out to Asbestos to see the strike first-hand and to meet his friend Jean Marchand, who by then was already a fabled union organizer and was the de facto strike leader.

The Asbestos Strike threw Trudeau at once into a political role that, like his personalism, provided a bridge between his old self and his new one, integrating his new interest in social democracy and individual freedom with his old commitment to freeing Quebec from the yoke of *les anglais*. But Duplessis himself was also a bridge: despite the close alliance between Duplessis and the Catholic Church that helped him keep a stranglehold on power, the Jesuits at Brébeuf had seen him as interloper, someone who had turned their own brand of socially oriented nationalism into one divorced from any real social commitment. In his play *Dupés,* John English notes, Trudeau had pilloried Duplessis in the character of Maurice Lesoufflé. Now it was through Duplessis—who always draped himself in the banner of nationalism but who called in the thugs and police who eventually broke up the strike—that Trudeau came to understand how Quebec nationalism often amounted to little more than a way for the elites to control the masses.

Though the strike was technically illegal, it garnered wide public support. In Montreal, Archbishop Joseph Charbonneau broke ranks with the church hierarchy and spoke out forcefully on the workers' behalf. In the end, however, the government forces came down hard, beating up resisters and making mass arrests, and the unions, after four months of bitter struggle, were forced to settle for a meagre pay increase. Many of the strikers never regained their jobs, and Charbonneau was forced to resign and was exiled to Victoria. Yet Trudeau would not be alone in seeing the strike as a turning point in Quebec. For once the public had taken a stand against the government on an issue of social justice, and a rift had opened up, however briefly, in the monolith of church and state.

Trudeau's main contribution to the strike was to offer free legal representation for workers who had been falsely imprisoned or had been intimidated or attacked by police. But it was his brief experience on the front lines, when he made the fiery speech that left Marchand disgruntled and joined the workers on the pickets, that most stayed with him. Coming as it did directly after his travels, it showed Trudeau how the world of oppression and poverty that he had experienced abroad was also right in his backyard. He had found a Quebec he had been unaware of, one "of workers exploited by management, denounced by government, clubbed by police, and yet burning with fervent militancy." His later writings about the strike were to be considered his finest.

On a practical level, however, his involvement in the strike had the effect of rendering him virtually unemployable in any government position in his home province. An application he made for a teaching position at the Université de Montréal was promptly turned down, despite his impeccable qualifications, and twice more over the decade that Duplessis was to continue in power Trudeau would apply for university positions and be refused. Marchand offered Trudeau work in the union movement, which would have been a logical fit, particularly as Trudeau had no need for a princely income. Instead, to the surprise of everyone, Trudeau left Montreal shortly after his work with the strike ended to take a job as a clerk in the Privy Council Office in Ottawa.

Trudeau's stated reason for leaving was his failure to get a teaching post. Yet the strike had shown that there was clearly a need in Quebec for someone with his talents. There may have been a part of him that balked at working in the trenches, where the chances to shine were so few, and where he could count not on the approval of his superiors, as in the past, but only on their condemnation. But a clerkship was hardly the place to make his name. It seemed, rather, that his first instinct on returning home was to flee again. Back in his old environment he must have felt a strange disjunction between his old self and his new one, between the old Quebec, which had seemed familiar and safe and unchanging, and one that looked very different in its sameness. The same elites, as he said, the sense of being mired in old ways of thinking, but also different despite itself, changed, like the rest of the world, by the war. Part of this change in Quebec was the collective amnesia that would have set in by then among all his old nationalist friends, one that would leave the fascistic excesses of their earlier nationalism unexamined for many years to come.

Trudeau, however, was not the sort to frame his decisions as *flights from* something, as much as they might be, but rather as *adventures into*. As challenges, in other words, and the challenge of Ottawa was a legitimate one. He was no longer one to take on an enemy at someone else's say-so; he would see for himself, as he had learned to do on his travels. In Israel, in the midst of a war, he had got himself smuggled into Jerusalem with a group of Arab soldiers after being turned away, though the adventure had landed him in an Arab prison for two days as an Israeli spy. In 1952, at the height of McCarthyism, he would travel to the Soviet Union for an economic conference, a trip that would briefly put him on the American blacklist. This insistence on forming his own opinions, on dealing with the other directly, would mark his years in power and would be what lay behind his very open relations with countries like Cuba, China, and the Soviet Union.

What he found in Ottawa was that it was not the citadel of evil it was often seen as in Quebec, but something rather

more human and also more narrow and mundane, particularly after London and Paris. Francophones, it was true, were
scarce and condescended to; English was the only language of
communication. If Trudeau excelled at everything he did, it
was no doubt partly to show his English superiors that he was
their equal. Yet in this supposed nest of vipers he also found
many good people to admire and respect. His boss was
Gordon Robertson, a career civil servant who would achieve
near-legendary status, serving under five prime ministers.
Robertson knew the value of having a French Canadian on
staff capable of dealing with constitutional issues and federal–provincial relations, and he gave Trudeau responsibilities
that went far beyond the usual ones for a junior clerk. At a
1950 constitutional conference in Ottawa, Trudeau also had a
chance to cross paths again with F.R. Scott, who attended the
conference as an adviser to Saskatchewan's CCF government.

Trudeau played his assigned role in Ottawa, adopting the
required neutrality of a civil servant and making dispassionate cases for all sides of an issue. On questions of federalism, however, he let his opinions come through,
consistently arguing against any encroachment on provincial
powers. Here in Ottawa he had a chance to witness in the
real world how the parts of a state worked together to form
a functioning whole, and that part of him that his friends

referred to as "his legalistic side" seemed to take great pleasure in trying to apply to Canada what he had learned in his studies abroad.

As anomalous as his departing for Ottawa had seemed, the two years he ended up spending there were likely pivotal in his agreeing a decade and a half later to run for federal office. They showed Trudeau not only that his studies could be applied directly to Canadian issues, but that Ottawa was a place neither to fear nor to loathe. He cut a swath there both professionally and socially: he was often seen about town with some beautiful young woman on his arm and found challenges that were sufficient to keep him engaged but were never beyond him. In the end, however, his argumentative nature began to chafe against the strictures imposed on civil servants. He did not always see eye to eye with the St. Laurent government, and he had particular problems with the external affairs minister of the time, who was none other than Lester Pearson. Trudeau, John English notes, was incensed at Pearson's support for the American-led intervention in the Korean War, seeing it as a mere aping of American Cold War policy. "Not a single original thought," Trudeau wrote to a colleague in External Affairs after hearing Pearson's speech on Korea in the House. "A little current history, a lot of propaganda."

Trudeau was rescued, finally, by *Cité libre,* which gave him both a reason to leave Ottawa and an excuse to, since he couldn't continue as a civil servant while publishing a polemical journal. There are varying stories about the origins of *Cité libre*—Trudeau himself claimed the idea went back to discussions in Paris after he and his Quebec friends heard that Duplessis had banned the film *Les enfants du paradis.* In any event, it was Gérard Pelletier who got the ball rolling while Trudeau was still in Ottawa. He pulled Trudeau into the project over the objections of many of his other recruits, who felt uneasy around Trudeau because of his background and his manner and his wealth. Trudeau's financial support, however, would end up keeping the journal afloat. Even at its height it would never have more than a few thousand readers, yet in the midst of the *Grande noirceur* of the Duplessis era it was one of the few rays of light. It was also where Trudeau himself was able to hone his ideas and to develop a firmness of conviction and clarity of thought that would later serve him well.

Cité libre provided Trudeau perhaps exactly the sort of vehicle he needed to re-enter the political world of Quebec, one suited both to his skills and to his temperament. It allowed him a public forum without requiring him to buy into any of the existing political structures, most of which he now had little respect for. The first issue of the journal contained an article whose title, "Politique fonctionelle," or functional politics, would come to define his own political stance over the next years. "We want to bear witness to the Christian and French fact in America. Fine; so be it. But let's get rid of all the rest." He was staking out the same territory as the nationalists, in others words, but not their methods. Rather, he was subjecting "to methodical doubt all the political categories relegated to us by the previous generation," such as the appeal to solidarity against the long list of imagined enemies, "communists, the English, Jews, imperialists, centralizers, demons, free-thinkers, and I don't know what else." This was a far cry from the rhetoric of the Trudeau of a mere six years earlier. It was as if he was shedding his old self, ready to start anew from first principles. "Let's batter down the totems, let's break the taboos. Better yet, let's consider them null and void. Let us be coolly intelligent."

This was the tone that *Cité libre* was to keep under Trudeau's reign. He had found an idiom, a way back to the language of protest he had always been most comfortable with, through an inversion that relegated what he himself had been to "the previous generation." Not a language of flight or remorse but of moving forward, of accepting a challenge. *Cité libre* would remain true to the challenge, tackling the federal government, the provincial one, even the church, despite the fact that the church, through its index of banned publications, had the power to shut the journal down.

In an article in one of the journal's early issues, Trudeau attacked the church's interference in secular affairs and poked fun at the "divine right" in which bishops cloaked themselves. The jibe provoked a caustic response in a Jesuit publication from one of Trudeau's favourite teachers at Brébeuf, Father Marie d'Anjou, as well as a summons for both Trudeau and Pelletier from the new Archbishop of Montreal, Paul-Émile Léger. Trudeau was rattled by the attack from d'Anjou, who had been one of his collaborators in *les X,* but at the meeting with Léger, who maintained a chilly diplomatic courtesy throughout, Trudeau refused to recant. Pelletier later described the encounter in his book *Years of Impatience.*

> Trudeau ... defended his position so sharply that the Archbishop was moved to say: "If I were to condemn the review ... it would be with great regret, believe me."
>
> "And we," interrupted Trudeau, "would appeal to the universal Church, as is our right."
>
> The Archbishop, disconcerted, stared strangely at Trudeau. He hesitated a moment, then went on to his next point. I have a lively recollec-

tion of those few moments during which, I believe, the fate of *Cité libre* was decided in the incredible atmosphere of a medieval dispute.

This sort of challenge required a rare strength of character in the Quebec of those years, particularly coming from someone who remained in his heart a committed Catholic. Yet despite Trudeau's many successes of this sort and the tremendous personal energies he put into *Cité libre,* to people around him he often seemed adrift in this period. His only other major projects during the 1950s were the collection of essays he put together, at Pelletier's request, on the Asbestos Strike, and a brief he prepared on behalf of the Quebec unions for a royal commission on federal–provincial relations. Interestingly, the brief, which actually garnered wide attention both in Quebec and in the rest of the country, took the view that economic issues were much more important than constitutional ones, and that workers needed adequate incomes more than they needed "constitutional guarantees of their religious, cultural, and political evolution." Many of Trudeau's critics in his latter years as prime minister, when Trudeau would keep hammering at constitutional reform while the deficit spiralled and interest rates and unemployment were in the double digits, might have made the same argument.

At the end of the decade, Trudeau, now forty, still seemed to have little to show for all the promise he had had as a young man. "Perhaps I seem superficial about certain things," Trudeau had written in his journal back at Brébeuf. "But the truth is that I work." This was as true of him in the 1950s as it had been at Brébeuf, but for all his activities, there was an air to him of someone who had never stepped fully into his own life. He was essentially jobless; he was unmarried. He might be in the midst of some project, then suddenly disappear on a months-long jaunt to Europe. He had become a frequent media commentator, on everything from politics to his hair-raising adventures abroad—this was the period in which Marshall McLuhan first noticed him—but this sort of exposure merely contributed to the impression that he was a dilettante. His forays into politics had been disillusioning: it seemed that no matter what tactics he and his fellow *Cité libre*-ists tried, whether they supported established opposition parties or set up parties or coalitions of their own, whenever elections rolled around, Duplessis always came out the victor. It wasn't just bribery and intimidation that kept him in power; it was that much of the electorate revered him, seeing in him exactly the sort of authority figure they had always looked to for leadership.

In retrospect, however, Trudeau and *Cité libre* came to be remembered as a focal point for reform-minded Quebecers of the time, and many of those who proved important in the Quiet Revolution got their introduction to politics in the intellectual milieu that coalesced around *Cité libre.* In the Quebec of the 1950s, this was no small accomplishment. This was a society that in one decade had had to live out a century of social evolution—and come to grips with the fact that it was not the self-sufficient peasant theocracy of its myths, but a modern, urban, industrialized society that could no longer hold out the forces of the greater world. The group that had formed around *Cité libre* was like a government-in-waiting, readying its program, biding its time until its moment came, and Trudeau was very much at the centre of it.

IT WAS AN IRONY that when the moment did come, it was not through the efforts of people like Trudeau but through Duplessis's sudden death in 1959, and then the sudden death of his promising successor, Paul Sauvé, shortly thereafter. By sheerest providence the solid ranks of the Union Nationale were unexpectedly split, and in June of 1960 the Liberals of Jean Lesage stepped into the breach and managed to scramble their way into power. In the next years, Lesage's

Quiet Revolution would transform Quebec. This was exactly the break Trudeau had been fighting for, yet almost at once he became one of the Revolution's most vocal critics.

By this point Trudeau had very clear ideas about the role of government in a democracy, along with an increasing appreciation of Canadian federalism. His only actual experience of Canada west of Ottawa at the time seems to have been on a family car trip in 1940, when he had been much more taken with the country's natural world than its human one, and yet the *idea* of Canada appealed to him. In *Federalism and the French Canadians,* Trudeau, in somewhat of a shift from his Privy Council days, still argued for respecting the constitutional division of powers, but suggested Canadian federalism had failed not in its giving too little power to Quebec but in its giving too much. Ideally, for him, federalism ought to have prevented exactly the Quebec situation of the 1950s: economic disparity, cultural isolation, and a province controlling powers it had no special aptitude for exploiting. What appealed to Trudeau, however, was that when properly administered, federalism could provide a very practical system of checks and balances, with centre and region each wielding the powers most suited to it, and with the opposition between them preventing either from exercising a tyrannical dominance.

Underlying Trudeau's arguments was his sense that it was only within a federal system that Quebec could avoid the risks inherent in ethnic nationalism. The sort of independent Quebec he had dreamed of as a young man, he saw now, would only have given greater rein to the ruling elites to exploit nationalism for their own ends, as Duplessis had done. In a Quebec obsessed with the survival of French-Canadian culture it was too easy for leaders to manipulate the electorate by promoting vague ideological goals rather than more practical ones, such as those of providing infrastructure and employment. A well-functioning federalism, on the other hand, could limit the appeal of this sort of demagoguery by ensuring protections against assimilation at the federal level as well as the provincial one.

In the ferment of the Quiet Revolution, however, such dispassionate views quickly began to seem out of step with the spirit of the times. The new crop of intellectuals, such as the founders of the journal *Parti pris*—who had initially looked to the *Cité libre*-ists as "our fathers," but who quickly parted ways with them—could not understand how Trudeau could continue to make such cold, logical arguments, with their legalistic niceties, in the face of what they saw as two hundred years of English oppression. Those who knew Trudeau well, of course, never described him as cold but rather as a man of deep feeling, even if he often hid it. "Let us be coolly intelligent," he had written in the first issue of *Cité libre,* and that had become his public stance, his mask. But the same issue had included heartfelt tributes from him to two thinkers recently dead, Léon Blum and Trudeau's old mentor, Harold Laski, "deux marxistes juifs" who had "distinguished themselves without cease by their intelligence, by their valiance, and by their tireless generosity." Bemoaning Canada's support for the Korean War and for America's Cold War logic, Trudeau praised Laski and Blum for being among those who had never subscribed to either of the totalitarianisms, but rather had "consecrated their lives to elaborating and agitating for a doctrine that advanced the cause of liberty, justice and peace. As was inevitable, they were hysterically denounced and hatefully reproached, as much by the orthodox Marxist camp as by the party of official Christianity."

The memorial to Laski must have had particular significance for Trudeau. Beneath his "coolly intelligent" mask, surely, was the memory of how his own, earlier totalitarianism had lessened his humanity, leading him to demonize others on the basis of race. Now Trudeau could hear the old language of ethnic nationalism beginning to creep into the rhetoric of the Lesage government. At the urging of Minister of Natural Resources René Lévesque—who had left his job as the popular host of a TV newsmagazine to join Lesage's Liberals—the government was proposing to nationalize Quebec's mainly English-owned hydroelectricity companies, which had long been a symbol for Quebecers of English domination. For Trudeau, the issue was not the proposal itself but the slogan under which it was being promoted: *maîtres chez nous,* masters in our own home. The new regime, even if it leaned left rather than right, was beginning to sound like the old one to Trudeau. Rather than making sound economic arguments for its actions, it was resorting to the old ideologies, using the familiar cry of repelling the enemy at the gates.

As the Lesage government grew more nationalistic, the new crop of young intellectuals grew more openly separatist in their beliefs and more revolutionary in their rhetoric. Trudeau was appalled to hear young people in universities speaking out against democracy or arguing for the necessity of totalitarianism during revolutionary movements. It all must have sounded familiar to him, though it must also have made him wonder if the province had taken a step forward only to take two back.

In a 1962 article in *Cité libre,* "The New Treason of the Intellectuals," Trudeau laid out in clear terms his objections to the separatists and the new nationalists, blaming ethnic-based nationalism for "the most devastating wars, the worst atrocities, and the most degrading collective hatred" of the previous two hundred years. All of Quebec's desired reforms, he argued, could be accomplished within the existing feder-ation. Once more he took the view that Quebec's focus ought to be on the pressing economic and practical issues facing the province. "A nation or people has only so much intellectual energy to spend on a revolution," he had said in his interview with Peter Gzowski. "If the intellectual energy of French Canada is spent on such a futile and foolish cause as separatism, the revolution that is just beginning here can never be brought about."

It was around this time that Trudeau fell in with a young man he would end up keeping close to him through the whole of his political career, Marc Lalonde. Lalonde had actually gone to Trudeau in Ottawa back in 1949, when he was twenty, to seek advice on his studies, just as Trudeau himself had sought advice a few years earlier from Henri Bourassa and André Laurendeau. Trudeau must have made an impression on Lalonde then, because in the early 1960s, Lalonde invited him to join a sort of think tank he and some like-minded friends had put together. Lalonde, by his own route, had come to some of the same conclusions as Trudeau about Quebec nationalism. He would also, by his own route, end up in Ottawa at the same time as Trudeau, hired on by Pearson as a constitutional adviser. Lalonde had done his graduate work at Oxford, during a period when it was a hotbed of radicalism, and he credited that period away from Quebec as having opened his mind to a much broader understanding of Quebec's place in the world, much as Trudeau's own studies abroad had done for him. It would be Lalonde who would give up his Christmas holiday in 1967 to set the wheels in motion for Trudeau's possible candidacy for the Liberal leadership, and it would be Lalonde who, as Pearson's constitutional adviser, would stage-manage Trudeau's role in the constitutional talks of early 1968 that would bring Trudeau such public prominence. It would also be to Lalonde, and not to Pelletier or Marchand, that Trudeau would turn for advice in February of that year, just before declaring his candidacy.

Together now with Trudeau, Lalonde's group produced a manifesto in 1964 in which the term *functional politics* again figured very prominently. If his province was moving backward, Trudeau himself must have felt as if he was standing still. Fourteen years after the launch of *Cité libre* he was still pushing the same platform, and was still no closer to realizing it. Change had happened in Quebec, dramatic change, and yet it seemed, just as Trudeau had predicted in an article in 1960, that French Canadians would "once again miss the turn."

Perhaps he was the one, however, who had missed the turn. At least he had been able to get a job now, teaching at the Université de Montréal, yet halfway into his forties he found himself a mere academic, for all the ambitions he had had. Even *Cité libre* was slipping from him, caught up in a factionalism to which his own anti-nationalist views had given rise. The moment had come for change, and he had not been part of it. When the chance had come to replace the Union Nationale after Duplessis's death, several of Trudeau's colleagues and friends had run for the Lesage Liberals as René Lévesque had. Trudeau, however, had been down in Key West during the campaign, attempting to paddle to Cuba in a homemade canoe. Lévesque later claimed that Trudeau, too, had been asked to run, but others said he had never been approached.

The academic Léon Dion, father of the future Liberal leader Stéphane, had once described Trudeau as Quebec's "most fascinating and disappointing intellectual of the 1950s." It must have looked to Trudeau as if the 1960s would serve him no better.

Then came the call from Jean Marchand.

CHAPTER FIVE

Just Watch Me

"An election is not a beauty contest," NDP Leader Tommy Douglas said after Trudeau's victory in 1968, echoing the feeling of many even within the Liberal Party that Trudeau had come to power more on show than on substance. There was plenty of truth to the charge, though part of Trudeau's success had come exactly from playing down his actual assets. In 1969, he told *The New Yorker* that he had "probably read more of Dostoevski, Stendhal, and Tolstoy than the average statesman, and less of Keynes, Mill, and Marx," even though he had read plenty of the latter three. This image of himself as being above the usual hurly-burly of politics had by then become part of his positioning. Already he was referring to himself as a "statesman" rather than a mere politician, a profession whose bad repute he had recognized all the way back in his play, *Dupés*.

The truth was that much less separated Trudeau from his two main rivals in the House, Douglas of the NDP and Robert Stanfield of the Progressive Conservatives, than met the eye. Stanfield was only five years his senior, and would outlive him, and both he and Douglas probably shared more general culture with Trudeau than Trudeau shared with the hippie generation he had become associated with. In Terence McKenna's 1994 documentary series on Trudeau, Trudeau admitted that he felt bad for Stanfield, who simply didn't have the right image for the times, but to whom he was probably more closely allied in both temperament and outlook than to the made-up Trudeau of Trudeaumania. As for Douglas, he was a much more logical political father for Trudeau than Pearson had been, and surely part of Trudeau's strategy of running more on image than substance had been to hide that fact.

Trudeau later said of the fans who had fuelled Trudeaumania that he wondered "how closely they were listening to my ideas, which sometimes I expounded rather dully." He had good cause to wonder, given that many of those fans, like the girls who had chased him up Parliament Hill, were teens still several years from voting age and couldn't have been much interested in theories of federalism. Within months of Trudeau's election, that sort of star-struck adulation had lost much of its currency and the media emphasis had already begun to shift from a kind of boosterism to a mix of voyeurism and censure. At a

Commonwealth conference in London early in 1969, Canadian reporters stalked Trudeau on his various forays into the city and on his dates with German jetsetter Eva Rittinghausen and actress Jennifer Hales, then filed stories suggesting he was spending more time living the life of the playboy than meeting his obligations as Canada's leader. At the end of the conference, Trudeau, just before rushing off to join Barbra Streisand and Princess Margaret for the London premiere of *Funny Girl,* gave reporters the first of the many tongue-lashings he was to administer to them over the years, lambasting them for their "crummy behaviour" and warning he might start prying into their lives as they had pried into his. "I think you once agreed when I said that the state has no place in the bedrooms of the nation; I could even say that the nation has no place in the bedrooms of the state, and certainly not the press." What seemed particularly to get Trudeau's goat was that reporters had tracked down Rittinghausen, who had given several indiscreet interviews before falling mum, and had hounded Hales to the point where she had left her apartment for several days. Ironically, the coverage Trudeau received turned him into an instant celebrity among Londoners and completely stole the thunder of the other heads of state gathered there.

Perhaps reporters devoted so much attention to Trudeau's social life because he failed to be especially controversial in his political one. At the conference, in the usual Canadian way, he set the tone for a constructive and peaceful discussion on the then tricky Rhodesia question, which had threatened to divide the conference on racial lines; and he reaffirmed Canada's strong commitment to the Commonwealth, though he had earlier called it an anachronism. There was a complaint from one delegate that he had been a disappointment after the high expectations people had of him and that he had done more observing than intervening; there was also a complaint from Canadian students he had met with that he put off several of their questions by saying he would have to consult with his ministers before reaching a decision. The divide between the image and the reality was starting to show: beneath his panache lurked a typical Canadian politician. A year or so into his first term an interviewer said to him that after the great changes people had hoped for from him, his government didn't seem to be doing much of anything. "I guess we're not doing anything if you call running the country not doing anything," Trudeau snapped back. The remark was less flippant than it sounded. For all his high talk about participatory democracy during the election and about "new guys with new ideas,"

Trudeau had some fairly basic, traditional notions about how government worked and about what it should do. As prime minister he was simply following the position he had always taken during his years at *Cité libre,* that it was much more important for government to tend to bread-and-butter issues than waste its energies on "revolution."

To the charge that his social activities cut into his political ones he might have answered as he had at Brébeuf: "The truth is that I work." Those who knew him on Parliament Hill, from his cabinet ministers, to his advisers, to his house staff at 24 Sussex, always attested, as his teachers had, to his discipline. It was well known that he liked his sleep and that he never arrived at the office early or left late. But he never went home without a package of work, and woe to the minister who arrived at a meeting the next day without having prepared for it as thoroughly as Trudeau himself had.

Unlike many of the prime ministers who preceded him, Trudeau required that all substantial issues come before the entire Cabinet for discussion rather than being simply presented as a *fait accompli* by the responsible ministry. The measure ensured a greater level of Cabinet involvement in major decisions, even if it meant not only more work for Cabinet members but a slower pace of decision-making and a burgeoning bureaucracy, as each department struggled to keep on top of issues from other departments. As it had been at the Commonwealth conference, Trudeau's preference was to observe discussion rather than dominate it and then to draw from what had emerged, a consensus style at odds with the common image of him as a man of set opinions with little tolerance for opposing views. Despite its drawbacks, Trudeau's system not only held true to his promise to make government more democratic but made a great deal of sense, allowing the accumulated experience and expertise of the government's senior members to be brought to bear on major questions. Since Trudeau's time most prime ministers have reverted to the close-fisted style of old, keeping a much tighter rein on decision making.

Only halfway into his first term, Trudeau, in what became known as the October Crisis, faced perhaps the most formidable challenge of his entire political career, and one that came to define him in the eyes of Canadians in terms much different from his previous "swinger" image. On October 5, 1970, British diplomat James Cross was kidnapped from his home in Montreal by the separatist Front de libération du Québec. Five days later, only hours after the Quebec government turned down the demands of Cross's captors, the FLQ struck again, kidnapping Trudeau's old schoolmate Pierre Laporte, now provincial labour minister in the Liberal government of Robert Bourassa, while he was playing football with his family on his front lawn. This second kidnapping, described in an FLQ communiqué as an act of retaliation for the government's intransigence, gave the impression of a high level of organization and sparked fears that the FLQ had embarked on a wide-ranging terror campaign.

The FLQ had been active in Quebec since 1963. Mainly a loose collection of "cells" that formed from time to time to carry out specific actions, it had no clear central leadership and an ideology that shifted through its various waves, at times narrowly nationalist and at others more broadly Marxist and revolutionary. One of its major figures, Pierre Vallières, had actually served as the editor of *Cité libre* in the early 1960s, as part of an effort to bring in a younger generation; Vallières had repaid the gesture by mocking the journal's founders and calling for revolution. By the mid-1960s Vallières had joined the FLQ and had been implicated in several bombings; his memoir *White Niggers of America*, written while he was in prison, had become the bible of the FLQ movement. Since its formation, the FLQ had been implicated in six deaths and in more than two hundred bombings in Quebec, including one in the Montreal Stock Exchange in 1969 that blew out a wall of the building and left twenty-seven injured. The kidnappings of Cross and Laporte in October 1970, the first use of this tactic, suggested that the FLQ had graduated to a more sophisticated level of terrorism.

Less than a year earlier, Prime Minister Trudeau had met with John Lennon and Yoko Ono, at their request, as part of their Crusade for Peace tour. After the meeting, Lennon concluded, "If all politicians were like Pierre Trudeau, there would be world peace." The October Crisis, however, would transform Trudeau's image in many people's minds from that of peace-loving hippie wannabe to one of cold, uncompromising autocrat. Much of that shift went back to a single twenty-second television clip in which young CBC reporter Tim Ralfe, eight days into the crisis, was seen confronting Trudeau on the steps of the Parliament Buildings, asking him about the sudden military presence on the Hill.

"There's a lot bleeding hearts around who just don't like to see people with helmets and guns," Trudeau said to him. "All I can say is go on and bleed. It's more important to keep law and order in this society than to be worried about weak-kneed people who don't like the looks of—"

"At any cost?" Ralfe interjected. "At any cost? How far would you go with that? How far would you extend that?"

Trudeau responded with the phrase that he would most be remembered for.

"Well, just watch me."

Three days later, the man who had been praised by John Lennon for his peaceful ways invoked the War Measures Act and turned the country into a virtual police state, suspending civil liberties and sending tanks and thousands of troops into the streets of Montreal. Quebec police initiated an immediate crackdown, arresting without charge hundreds of supposed FLQ sympathizers—including well-known writers, entertainers, labour leaders, and members of the Parti Québécois—the vast majority of whom turned out to have no link to the crisis. The day after the measures were introduced, as if in direct retaliation for them, Pierre Laporte was discovered strangled to death in Montreal in the trunk of a car after an anonymous call to a local radio station.

At the time, there was overwhelming support in both Quebec and the rest of Canada for Trudeau's hard-line stance, though in the following months and years, particularly as information began to emerge about police abuses not only at the time but both before and after the crisis, public attitudes began to shift, especially in Quebec. Most damning were the revelations that the RCMP had carried out a number of actions after the crisis to indicate continuing

FLQ activity, including issuing false FLQ communiqués, stealing dynamite, and infamously burning down a barn that belonged to an imprisoned FLQ member's mother, in an incident that was to become a symbol of RCMP perfidy. Given that anti-terrorist police had so infiltrated the FLQ by that point as to constitute virtually its only members, the RCMP activities seemed aimed not at terrorism but at discrediting the separatist movement as a whole and in particular the Parti Québécois, whose membership lists the RCMP stole in 1973 from the party offices in an action they called Operation Ham.

Trudeau correctly predicted that the murder of Pierre Laporte would be the death knell of the FLQ, which in fact completely lost public support afterwards. But the killing was not the death of separatism. On the contrary, the October Crisis seemed to push the separatist movement toward political maturity. Separatism was now able to present itself as a peaceful alternative to the FLQ while still drawing on the underlying support for the FLQ's objectives and on the memory of federal troops occupying the streets of Montreal. Trudeau's "Just watch me" began to seem more and more the epitome of the arrogance of the federal government, which was willing to ride roughshod over the aspirations of the Quebec people in order to safeguard its own power. In English Canada, meanwhile, the statement came to represent the betrayal of the ideals that the 1960s generation had invested in Trudeau, who was now revealing himself as merely another pillar of the establishment.

The actual details of the October Crisis, however, give a much more nuanced impression of Trudeau's role. Trudeau's "Just watch me" interview, for instance, reads completely differently when seen in its entirety than it does in the provocative clip that it got reduced to by most of the media. The exchange between Ralfe and Trudeau actually went on some seven and a half minutes and was more in the way of a spirited debate than an interview. What comes across in Trudeau is not so much a sense of arrogance as of generosity. In all the tension of the moment, with the troops swarming the hill and the crisis in its eighth day, he stopped to give Ralfe his undivided attention, openly soliciting his opinions and on more than one occasion ignoring the questions of other reporters clamouring for attention around them. Ralfe had managed to catch Trudeau's interest by raising a legitimate question: what was the appropriate use of force in a democracy? Much of what comes across as belligerence in the shortened piece sounds merely like the usual Trudeau hyperbole in the full interview. On the whole, Trudeau got the better of Ralfe, presenting a logical defence for his actions to which his "Just watch me" was simply a punchy conclusion. As he continued on his way, he gave Ralfe a smile and a pat on the shoulder and commended him on playing the devil's advocate.

Trudeau's behaviour during the crisis, in fact, showed very little bravado and a good deal of integrity and restraint. From the beginning he took the position that there should be no capitulation to the terrorists' demands—which included the release of so-called "political prisoners"—on the legitimate grounds that conciliation would only encourage further terrorist acts. In future years, this logic would in fact come to define the official response to terrorism around the world. Trudeau was as good as his word; at the time he even made it clear in private to his future wife, Margaret, whom he was already secretly seeing, that he would take the same line even if she or one of their children were ever to be kidnapped.

In Quebec, Premier Bourassa at first under-reacted to the crisis, failing to cancel an official visit to New York after Cross was kidnapped, and then instantly went into a siege mentality after the Laporte kidnapping, holing up his entire Cabinet in a Montreal hotel under strict security. Meanwhile Mitchell Sharp, the external affairs minister, had, without Trudeau's permission, agreed to let the abductors' manifesto be read on air, believing it was so scattered and extreme that it could only hurt the FLQ cause. The tactic backfired: students in Quebec immediately began to express sympathy with the kidnappers' demands and to organize rallies and protests in support of the FLQ. In addition, a petition signed by sixteen prominent Quebec personalities, including labour leaders, businessmen, academics, and Trudeau's old associates René Lévesque, now leader of the fledgling Parti Québécois, and Claude Ryan, at the time editor of *Le Devoir,* called on the Quebec government to negotiate with the abductors "despite and against all obstruction from outside of Quebec."

Bourassa, however—who at many important moments over the course of his career would suffer a failure of nerves—had neither the will nor the desire to face the crisis alone and implored Trudeau to send in troops to assist his police in tracking down the abductors. Rumours abounded of arms caches, of bomb threats, of further FLQ cells planning further abductions, and Bourassa apparently feared that the province was on the verge of revolution. Under the National Defence Act, Trudeau was legally obliged to meet Bourassa's request for troops. But the decision whether to accede to Bourassa's further request for the special powers available under the War Measures Act was Trudeau's alone.

The act would amount to a total suspension of civil liberties, allowing for searches without warrant and detentions without charge. It could only be invoked, however, in the case of "war, invasion or insurrection, real or apprehended."

It later came out that in Cabinet Trudeau had initially been against imposing the act, not trusting that the information coming from police and from the provincial government was reliable and being wary of the political fallout of imposing such far-reaching measures. It was a young minister from Quebec, however, Jean Chrétien, whose philosophy carried the day. "Act now," was his advice, "explain later." What finally tipped Trudeau toward imposing the act was the petition signed by his former colleagues, which had uncritically adopted the term *political prisoners* from the FLQ list of demands. In Trudeau's eyes, this legitimizing of the terrorists' rhetoric—the prisoners in question had been convicted of criminal acts that included bombings and manslaughter—showed that even the elite in Quebec had lost all perspective. To protect himself, however, Trudeau insisted that Bourassa and Mayor Jean Drapeau of Montreal—the same person for whom Trudeau had given his rousing anti-conscription speech back in 1942—write letters requesting emergency powers and making specific reference to a state of insurrection.

In the House, the only dissenter when Trudeau announced the act was Tommy Douglas, who accused the government of using "a sledgehammer to crack a peanut." He turned out to be right. All of the abductors were eventually revealed to be well known to police—who might easily have prevented the kidnappings if they had bothered to follow through on their own information, which included repeated reports from one of their informants that a major FLQ action was in the offing. After sixty days, the location where Cross was being held was tracked down through normal police work, and his release was negotiated in exchange for his abductors' free passage to Cuba. The killers of Laporte, meanwhile, again through normal police work, were all arrested within two and a half months of the killing. No evidence was ever discovered of an arms cache or of any organized plan for insurrection. The taking of Laporte, in fact, had been merely an in-sympathy action, planned at the last moment, given that the only information the two cells initially had of each other's activities was what they had read in the papers. The Cross kidnappers later admitted that the Laporte kidnapping had been a mistake: by implying a much higher level of organization than was the case, it had essentially been responsible for the authorities' exaggerated reaction.

Even the killing of Laporte involved a level of happenstance. At the time it seemed a direct retaliation for the imposition of the War Measures Act, but according to the admission long afterwards of one Laporte's abductors, Francis Simard, it was more a matter of last resort. Laporte, who the day after his abduction was allowed to send a letter to Bourassa in which he pleaded for his life, apparently grew severely depressed as his captivity continued. On hearing about the imposition of the act on his abductors' TV, he tried to escape by flinging himself at a window, botching the attempt but seriously injuring himself in the process. His abductors were then faced with the prospect of his bleeding to death if he didn't receive medical help and in the end decided to kill him, strangling him with his own necklace, according to Simard, because they couldn't bear the thought of the "fascists" having the victory.

It would be years, however, before the various inquiries that looked into the kidnappings would report their findings and before the kidnappers themselves would publicly admit any of the specifics of what had happened. Many conspiracy theories would be alleged, a few backed up by actual evidence, and many people's positions would shift depending on convenience and the political winds. Bourassa would later say he had called for the War Measures Act not because he had truly believed an insurrection was imminent but so he could say he had taken every possible action—an admission that only seemed to highlight his lack of leadership in the crisis. Robert Stanfield, who had supported the measures, later regretted that he had, as did several of Trudeau's cabinet ministers of the time. Even Jean Marchand, who had claimed during the crisis that the FLQ had thousands of active members and hundreds of pounds of dynamite, later said the act had been "like using a cannon to kill a fly."

Trudeau himself was never to recant. In his memoirs, however, he went to uncharacteristic lengths to defend his actions, which suggested he had taken the criticism over them to heart. Part of the reason, no doubt, was that the crisis had been such a personal one for him. In retrospect it got cast as the usual battle between Ottawa and Quebec, but for Trudeau, only two years in power then, it would have been a much more internal battle, fought entirely on his home turf. People like Ryan and Lévesque with whom he had once shared common purpose were now his enemies; he saw the lists of people arrested as a result of the act and knew the names. Back at Brébeuf he had sat in the desk next to Pierre Laporte's; a generation earlier their fathers had also been schoolmates. Meanwhile, the FLQ, which for most Canadians was a faceless entity they knew only from the nightly news, for Trudeau meant young men like Pierre Vallières, who had passed through the very offices of *Cité libre*, and who must have seemed as impassioned and wrong-headed as he himself had once been. In one of the ironies of the crisis, Jacques Lanctôt, one of Cross's abductors, and Paul Rose, leader of the cell that kidnapped Laporte, had first met in a police van after being arrested at the 1968 Saint-Jean-Baptiste protest that had brought Trudeau such renown. Rose later said it was that event that had radicalized him and turned him to the FLQ.

The kidnappers all ended up doing their time. Even those who had been given free passage to Cuba eventually grew bored there and returned home of their own accord, to be tried and imprisoned. In 1981, however, the Laporte kidnapper Jacques Rose, Paul's brother, by then already paroled, was given a standing ovation at a convention of the Parti Québécois. The one dissenter was René Lévesque, who had served with Laporte in the Lesage government and who looked visibly dumbfounded at Rose's warm reception. Lévesque's reaction underlined what had become by then the peculiar, complex legacy of the October Crisis. Though Lévesque had given nearly two decades to the separatist cause by then and had staked much of his political capital on the failed referendum of the previous year, he could, nevertheless, see how the lens of nationalist sentiment had already distorted his party's collective memory of Rose's actions. For many in Quebec, however, despite the overwhelming approval there of Trudeau's handling of the crisis at the time, the event had somehow become a symbol of his betrayal of the Quebecois. In English Canada, too, it came to be seen as a moment of reversal, when Trudeau had abandoned the principles that people had admired in him and shown himself a despot.

The revelations from the Trudeau archives of his fascistic prewar attitudes might suggest he had merely reverted, during the crisis, to an old, authoritarian self. It would be easier to argue, however, that if his old self ever crossed his mind during the crisis, it was surely in horror. The abductors were what he had been, this handful of militants determined to overthrow the established order—except that they had acted. He was seeing now, from the other side, what he might have become but what all the intervening years had turned him away from. His actions during the crisis, far from betraying his principles, had sprung from them: he had upheld the rule of law. Whatever knowledge he may have had in later years of the RCMP's nefarious operations to discredit the separatists, the evidence suggests that at the time of the October Crisis, at least, he acted in good faith. Of the many players in the drama—Premier Bourassa and the police, the petition signers and flame-fanners, the kidnappers themselves—Trudeau, arguably, behaved the most clear-headedly, again the right man at the right moment.

For all the criticism Trudeau took over the matter afterwards, his handling of the crisis became an indelible part of his image and likely helped account both for his political longevity and for his continuing place in the Canadian consciousness long after his retirement. He was the man who spoke his mind. Who was strong when he needed to be. The impeccable logic he brought to his uncompromising treatment of the kidnappers—give in and there would be no end—was the same logic he would bring to the constitutional talks and to his attacks, after his retirement, on the Meech Lake and Charlottetown accords. It was a logic born again of the legalistic mind that his detractors scoffed at and that in his public image often read as something quite different: arrogance, bravado, wilfulness, though also as strength, which people responded to. Whatever else Trudeau did during the October Crisis, he didn't make a botch of it. He didn't dither. He didn't embarrass us before the eyes of the world, but gave a grave situation its proper gravity. For that, we were grateful.

Trudeau's exchange with Tim Ralfe on the steps of Parliament during the crisis contrasts sharply with the self-protective sound bytes favoured by today's politicians. In the midst of a crisis he was willing to be put to the test, to stand in front of the nation and risk the extravagant statement, the rhetorical flourish. It was a quality that drew the public's eye to him. There was always the sense in an interview with Trudeau that there was no script, that anything might happen. Part of that feeling came from the fact that he was as much the questioner as the questioned, that he, too, was putting out a challenge.

Over the years Trudeau came to be seen as increasingly hostile to the media, but the truth was likely more complex. An intensely private man, he nonetheless never got out of the habit of taking planeloads of journalists with him whenever he travelled, and many of his diatribes against them seemed to have come from a desire not so much to be free of them as to improve them, to make them understand the seriousness of the task they were involved in. At the Commonwealth conference in London, when he had threatened to pry into journalists' private lives as they had pried into his, his point had been that they, too, were public figures with public responsibilities.

The media never quite lived up to Trudeau's standards, yet at some level he must have understood that much of what he was, much of what he was seen to be, he owed to them. "I'm kind of sorry I won't have you to kick around anymore," he said, parodying Nixon, when in 1979 he announced what he thought would be his retirement. But there seemed real affection in the jibe. Some ten years earlier, when Trudeau was still in his honeymoon phase, Barbara Frum had asked Patrick Watson, "When Trudeau talks to you, Patrick, who's more in control, you or Trudeau?" The truth, perhaps, as in the interview with Norman DePoe, was neither. It was, rather, that quality in Trudeau, as Marshall McLuhan had seen, that said, "Just watch me."

In the short term, Trudeau's ratings reached their highest levels after the October Crisis, though they did not stay there long enough to spare him near-humiliation in the election of 1972. In the interim, however, he would have a second honeymoon with the Canadian public, and his first private one, when his marriage to the woman on whose shoulder he had secretly wept at the death of Pierre Laporte, Margaret Sinclair, would briefly return him to the glory of the days of Trudeaumania.

CHAPTER SIX

In the Bedrooms of the Nation

Trudeau's secret marriage to Margaret Sinclair on March 4, 1971, broke many hearts and started a chapter in Trudeau's life that for some time to come would provide exactly the sort of copy in the international press that Trudeau had always abhorred, even as a part of him seemed to court it. The few short years that the marriage encompassed were in some ways a defining period both for Trudeau himself and for the country. Many people who couldn't name a single Trudeau policy initiative from the 1970s can still remember what Maggie wore when she met the Queen, or which head of state's wife she composed a poem for, or what infant child she had with her on the visit to Fidel Castro. By the time of her infamous weekend with the Rolling Stones a mere six years after her marriage, she had left the country with a sense of having forever shed its image as a bad mix of staid Presbyterianism and priest-ridden Catholicism. She had also left Pierre with three sons, two born Christmas Day, who would make him seem in his later years the perfect family man even as he reverted to his days of swinging bachelor-hood.

The daughter of a former Liberal cabinet minister, Margaret had met Trudeau briefly in Tahiti during Christmas 1967. They had discussed Plato then, she said afterwards, though Trudeau had not made much of an impression on her, her attention being taken up with a handsome young Frenchman named Yves. It was not until two years later, when, as prime minister, he showed up in Vancouver and took her out on a date, that she was stricken. "Call me up if you're ever in Ottawa," he said, a line he had apparently used more than once, and overnight Margaret decided to abandon her search for hippiehood, move to Ottawa, and apply for a government job. Trudeau may have been a bit shocked when this waif to whom he had issued a casual invitation suddenly showed up at his doorstep having thrown over her entire life. What started out as an on-again, off-again dalliance, however, slowly took on the rhythm of an actual relationship. In Margaret's version of things Trudeau never actually proposed to her, merely put the idea of marriage before her as a matter of negotiation. He set some tasks: she had to prove she could remain faithful, and she had to give up dope. After she had gone several months without a joint or a sexual lapse, the date was set, and on March 5, 1971, the country learned, with some giddiness, that their perpetual-bachelor prime minister had tied the knot. From the outside, the whole matter had the air of a storybook marriage, though as it came to unravel in the following years the storybook image would give way to a tabloid one that proved all the more riveting.

Trudeau was fifty-one when he married, and Margaret Sinclair, a mere twenty-two then, was hardly his first love. Margaret's contention that he was reluctant to marry her because he thought she would leave him has the ring of truth: for all the image of Trudeau as someone afraid to commit, in the few great romances of his life it had always been the woman who had ended the relationship. This was the case, in a sense, even with the woman who was arguably the first true love of his life, his mother, Grace, who had remained a central presence in his life well into the 1960s. While Grace Trudeau kept almost no records of her own life or of her husband's, she was as scrupulous an archivist of Pierre's life, according to John English, as he himself would be in his early years, keeping detailed records of his progress from the day of his birth and continuing to build her archive on him into her dotage. Right from Pierre's earliest years she had had high hopes for him, and after her husband's death he became the focus of her attentions and her closest confidant and companion. Whenever he was away she kept up a steady correspondence with him. "Every time the postman comes I make a rush for the letters, hoping to hear from you," she wrote him the year he was studying in Paris. That spring she joined him there and toured the south of France with him on the back of his Harley-Davidson.

By the time Pierre met Maggie, however, Grace had also essentially abandoned Trudeau, already suffering from dementia. In *Beyond Reason,* Margaret spoke of Grace with great fondness, giving her the credit for Trudeau's turning out "as generous, tolerant and understanding as he is." Most of her impressions of Grace, however, would necessarily have had to come to her through Trudeau, and some of Trudeau's earlier loves, whose experience of Grace had been more firsthand, had not been quite so well disposed to her. "'Formidable' is the word Trudeau sometimes uses to describe his father," Richard Gwyn observed in *The Northern Magus.* "Everyone else applies it to his mother." Trudeau himself always praised his mother for the tremendous freedom she allowed him, but while she may never have openly disapproved of any of his relationships, her shadow always loomed behind them. "It was something of a shock to me as well as to you," she wrote to Pierre when she learned one of the great loves of his life had broken off with him. "When I realized how serious was the rift, especially as I had begun to take the girl to heart—which requires time for such an adjustment! Blood is thicker than water you know I often say."

John English gives a rich portrait of Trudeau's early loves in *Citizen of the World,* one that reveals a man rather at odds with the Casanova figure he would often later be seen as. "I don't want to go out with girls before I am twenty years old because they would distract me," he wrote in his journal at Brébeuf, but then at eighteen he fell in love with a Franco-American girl, Camille Corriveau, whom he had met at Old Orchard Beach in Maine, where the family vacationed. Pierre shared his first kiss with Camille, but their relationship was decidedly puritan by contemporary standards, consisting mainly of letters and brief summer encounters. This was the first of several of Trudeau's relationships that would be primarily epistolary and intellectual rather than carnal. Camille eventually fell in love with and married a fellow Franco-American and her relationship with Pierre shifted into mere friendship, another pattern that would repeat itself. Grace called on Camille in New England some years later while visiting Pierre's brother Tip at Harvard and reported cattily back to Pierre that she was up to her ears in diapers with "no help from outside—does all her own work."

By then, however, Trudeau was already in hot correspondence with the woman he seemed destined for, Thérèse Gouin, the daughter of a Liberal senator and the descendant of a long line of progressive French-Canadian politicians that included two former Quebec premiers. Attractive, well educated, wealthy, ambitious, and fluently bilingual, she was a match for both Trudeau's intelligence and his social class, and was considered suitable marriage material, Clarkson and McCall note in *Trudeau and Our Times,* even by Trudeau's "notoriously sniffy" mother. For two years Trudeau wrote letters to her from Harvard of increasing ardour and intensity, confessing his love as well as his own loneliness and self-doubt. Yet he had already made arrangements to study in Paris by the time he finished at Harvard, then spent half of the intervening summer, astoundingly, not in Montreal with his beloved but working at a gold mine in Abitibi. Thérèse, a psychology student, must have seen red flags in every direction. In Paris Trudeau began to see a psychoanalyst, but then grew jealous of the analysis Thérèse herself was undergoing as part of her training. According to Clarkson and McCall, Trudeau had made clear to Thérèse by then his resolutely traditional expectations of a wife: someone who would sacrifice her own ambitions in order to "manage his household affairs prudently, and raise his children wisely." Thérèse, who clearly had no intention of sacrificing herself, grew more sparing in her correspondence, delivering the *coup de grâce* when Trudeau returned to Montreal the following summer. Trudeau took the blow hard. By now he was nearly twenty-eight, and, as his notes from his analysis show, he was still a virgin.

BACK IN HIS EARLY TWENTIES, Trudeau had outlined a strategy for his future relations with women. "I must continually work for perfection and become likable, obliging, and gallant (what a word!)." It would be some years before he managed to get the strategy right. For all his casual playboy image in later life, his early relationships were all marked by an intensity and need that inevitably led to their demise.

It was in Ottawa, during his time with the Privy Council, that the first signs of the later Trudeau style began to emerge. After the *Ottawa Citizen,* clearly at a loss for hard news, ran a front-page article on a twenty-year-old Swedish bombshell just hired on at the Swedish Embassy who spoke five languages and had studied French literature at Lausanne, Trudeau set out to woo her. His commitment to chastity had apparently ended by then, and within a matter of months he and Helen Segerstrale were an item and she was sending him *billets-doux* from the embassy signed "Puss." "I feel like a young debutante, who has the love of a young man who must write sentimental things to the object of his great desire." When they began to talk seriously of marriage, however, fault lines appeared in the relationship. Trudeau's mother took it upon herself to help Helen in the matter of her conversion to Catholicism, which for Pierre was a nonnegotiable precondition to their marriage. Helen was not averse but found there was some difference between the personalist Catholicism that Pierre talked about and the priestly Catholicism that still reigned in Quebec. Meanwhile Pierre, characteristically, chose this moment to quit his job and set off for Europe. He had arranged to meet Helen in Gibraltar, but Helen never showed, sending a Dear John letter instead: she had met someone new. "My love, I love you," she had written earlier, "I always have and always will to the end of the world. My love, is this itself not enough? Evidently not, because you seem to say that I don't express my love well enough or often enough."

This was to be Trudeau's last serious brush with marriage until he met Margaret. From this point on the playboy image took over, and the women in his life became less girlfriends than "companions." There would be a number of these women over the years, both before and after Margaret, in relationships that might stretch on for years but that often overlapped with other ones, frequently to the women's surprise. "I don't remember why I became a bachelor," he would tell Norman DePoe. "It happened so long ago that I don't think I could tell you." Over the course of his life he would have far greater success with bachelorhood than he would ever have with marriage, though even women who knew him in his later years would say that his conquests were not quite so extensive as his public image suggested. As Margot Kidder put it:

> I know morality is not much in fashion these days, but Pierre was someone who just could not give up the habit. And anyway, you always sensed with him that his own heart had been broken way, way back down the line by *someone*—a woman, his father perhaps, a cruel school chum—and he had vowed to not pass on his infection.

Two women he would grow very close to in the years before Margaret were Carroll Guérin and Madeleine Gobeil. Guérin was an artist and model who was frequently seen with Trudeau through the late 1950s and into the 1960s and to whom Trudeau was attracted for exactly the sort of independence and unconventionality he seemed unable to tolerate in a prospective spouse. By now, however, Trudeau had learned to curb the precipitous intensity that had spelled the end of his earlier relationships. Correspondence again played its part, as he and Guérin often found themselves on different continents, though they spent a happy summer together in Rome and on the Riviera in the early 1960s. Afterwards Guérin moved to England, but while Trudeau visited her there and continued to write to her during his first years in Ottawa, the relationship never seemed to move beyond its initial open-endedness.

Madeleine Gobeil was a starstruck eighteen-year-old when she met Trudeau at a political meeting in Ottawa in 1957. Trudeau gave her short shrift then, but when she turned up at a book launch of his in the early 1960s she was no longer a tongue-tied adolescent. In a 1963 *Maclean's* roundtable, Peter Gzowski described Gobeil as "serious, clever, frank and, above all, emancipated. She is, for example, unafraid to say publicly that she no longer believes in her church." Trudeau's relationship with Gobeil was another that would span the years and the continents, ending abruptly only with Trudeau's marriage. After a stint in Paris in the mid-1960s, where Gobeil made a name for herself with her journalism, including an interview with Jean-Paul Sartre that was published in *Playboy,* she was hired by Carleton University to teach French literature and was often seen with Trudeau during his first years in government. His marriage to Margaret, however, was a shock. Within months she had left Ottawa and returned to Paris, where she took a job with UNESCO and refused to see Trudeau again until after his divorce.

If there was a common factor in the significant women in Trudeau's life who preceded Margaret, it was that all of them, in great measure, appeared to be suitable matches for him. If these women were also beautiful—"Interestingly, Trudeau, a relatively small, very thin, though strongly muscled man," John English notes, "was attracted to beautiful, full-figured, and tall women"—then Trudeau had worked hard enough at his own physique to have earned that perk. The most striking aspect of the young Margaret Sinclair in the context of this lineage was how woefully unqualified— aside from her looks—she was to follow in it. She was a mere nineteen when Trudeau met her in Tahiti, and only twenty-two to his fifty-one when he married her. And apart from an undergraduate degree from Simon Fraser University, where she had studied political science, sociology, and anthropology, she had few of the accomplishments and none of the refinements that Trudeau had previously favoured. After graduation she had spent several months wandering, at her parents' expense, through Morocco, where excessive drug use and sex had brought her no closer to the enlightenment she had set out in search of. By the time she landed back on her parents' doorstep in the Vancouver suburbs in the summer of 1969 she was without plans and without hopes.

All that changed when the prime minister asked her out on a date.

What was it in Margaret that was to capture the world's attention so? Somehow, though in a more undisciplined way, she had the same "Just watch me" quality that Trudeau had, this flower child in her muslin tops and flowing skirts whose next step, like Trudeau's, you could never predict. At the Liberal Convention in 1968, which Margaret's family attended because her father was an organizer for John Turner, Trudeau remembered Margaret at once from their brief meeting in Tahiti, picking her out of the mob that surrounded him after his victory and going over to kiss her on both cheeks, as if anointing her. Over the next years we would watch her as we did Trudeau, seeing in her the same fairy-tale quality of having been plucked from nowhere into greatness. We watched her because she seemed so unlikely;

because we feared and hoped for some gaffe; because we did not know—and it seemed often enough that she herself did not know—what she would do next. We watched her because the camera loved her. The media made her, as it had made Trudeau: just as with him, there were iconic images of Margaret that would be etched in the Canadian psyche. Margaret in her white wedding garb on the cover of *Time,* Trudeau doting behind her. Margaret and Pierre swinging Sacha through an airport corridor. Margaret with the Queen. Margaret with Castro. Margaret with Justin, then Sacha, then Micha.

Just as the media had made her, however, so it unmade her. Partying all night with the Rolling Stones in Toronto. Dancing at Studio 54 while her husband went down to defeat at the polls. A famous photo of Margaret caught pantyless seemed the nadir, but there was more to come, as she launched a B movie career that included a bodice-ripper whose script was written by a gynecologist. By then Margaret had begun to seem a grotesque inversion of Trudeau: where he had put walls, she had put windows, injudiciously baring herself to a world that was all too happy to take whatever she offered. The unravelling of her story was as mesmerizing, in its way, as its coming together had been, and maybe as satisfying: just as we had all lived vicariously through her apotheosis, we were now comforted in our conventionality by her downfall.

The real story of Maggie and Pierre, however, was not particularly glamorous or remarkable. Much of it we know through Margaret's own books, *Beyond Reason* and *Consequences,* which were considered in bad taste when they came out but were actually a model of discretion with regard to Trudeau himself. No revelations of bedroom quirks or of some monster or petty tyrant who lurked behind the charm, no bitter recriminations or flinging of blame. On the contrary, her comments about Trudeau tended less to soil his public image than to soften it, as they had when she had joined Trudeau on the campaign trail, against the wishes of his advisers, in the election of 1974. Speaking to an audience in Vancouver then, she had called Trudeau "a beautiful guy" who "taught me everything I know about loving."

There was very little in the books to contradict this image. "Pierre is one of the gentlest of men, a loving father and a very loyal friend," she wrote of him, taking most of the blame for the failure of the marriage on herself. Trudeau's own culpability came out mainly as a sort of benign inattentiveness: his holding court entirely in French at a dinner party without realizing that Margaret didn't speak it; his failure to notice the chilly refusal of the domestic staff at

24 Sussex to relinquish any control of the household to her. In the end her life came apart so spectacularly and so indiscreetly that the public, too, would tend to spare Trudeau any of the blame for the marriage's failure.

Here was a man, however, who had chosen for his wife someone thirty years his junior and who shared none of his accomplishments or learning or experience. It was not as if he lacked options. Why choose Margaret over someone like his long-time "companion" Madeleine Gobeil, who was still living in Ottawa when he was secretly dating Margaret and who was someone much more suited to him in age and accomplishments than Margaret was? Though the marriage was seen as another example of Trudeau's bucking of convention, the truth was likely much different. In *Consequences,* in a tone slightly less genial than that of her first book, Margaret described the three categories women fell into for Trudeau:

> There were his female colleagues, and these he saw only as working companions and not as women, though many were also close friends. Then there were possible dates and here, like Edward VIII, he preferred actresses and starlets, glamorous women who were perfect for flirtations and candlelight dinners. Then there was his wife, and she had to be dependent, at home, and available.

Margaret might have added "pregnant," which she was for almost half of her marriage to Trudeau. Trudeau had always wanted children, and he had always been envious of friends who had married at the proper age and had growing broods while he was still living at home like an adolescent. His earlier relationships had failed not so much because of his aversion to the strictures of domestic life but exactly because he had been attracted to women of accomplishment who had much less traditional views of women's roles than he had. For all the emphasis throughout his life on human rights, Trudeau, in practical terms, never showed himself to be much of a feminist. In an interview with Gloria Steinem in 1969, he was visibly awkward, stumbling in his response to her charge that there was a dearth of women in his government and attempting to take refuge in a gallantry that made him look decidedly old-fashioned next to Steinem.

Margaret, however, was not Gloria Steinem—or Thérèse Gouin. She had no projects or ambitions outside of her marriage and openly admitted that she "planned to get pregnant as soon as I could." No one was ever to suggest Trudeau married Margaret for anything other than love, yet there was something coldly practical in the arrangement—in his putting the idea of marriage forward as if he were presenting a government white paper; in his setting of tasks. It was as though the pattern he had begun in the 1950s of casual relationships with interesting women had been a way of resolving the contradiction his earlier relationships had foundered on, that the independence and accomplishment that stimulated him in a lover he could not have accepted in a wife. Apparently the man who sought challenges in every other sphere of his life did not want to feel challenged in his marriage.

In the end, Margaret proved one of his largest challenges, and one of the few at which he would fail. His inattentiveness was likely much less benign than Margaret generously suggested in her books: it left her to flail. "Pierre's nature was such that he wasn't able to help me," she wrote, by which she meant that his idea of attending to her was to give her a car and her own phone line. However much of "a beautiful guy" he was, he saw his principal role during their marriage as that of prime minister, and not that of giving on-the-job training in how to be a prime minister's wife.

In *Beyond Reason,* Margaret recounted that when she was packing up to leave Pierre in 1977 she found a note she had written only a year and a half after their marriage, when their son Justin was just nine months old. "I am so lonely. I should be happy. I am married to a man who loves me and I have a wonderful baby. But I am terribly unhappy." Five years and two sons later she was still unhappy, and for largely the same reasons. At twenty-two she had been as unformed as Trudeau himself had been at twenty-two, but while Trudeau had had the luxury of the next twenty-odd years to prepare for the scrutiny of the world, Margaret had had to learn under its glare. For much of her life at 24 Sussex her only respite was the room she had arranged for herself in the attic, painted canary yellow, where she could retreat between run-ins with the domestic staff and the plots by Trudeau insiders to undermine her and the media moments when she wore the wrong dress to a White House dinner or wrote an embarrassing poem for the First Lady of Venezuela.

Margaret reserved particular scorn in *Beyond Reason* for those Trudeau staffers who seemed determined from the start to keep her from horning in on their sphere of influence. On the campaign trail in 1974, her "old adversary" Ivan Head, Trudeau's speech writer and foreign policy adviser, "did his best to ease me out," she wrote, "creating an indefinable but unmistakable aura that I was totally redundant on the trip. He was always smiling, always whispering something in Pierre's ear, and I felt moments of pure childish jealousy." By all accounts, Margaret's perception of what Richard Gwyn called "the manipulative character of life in the court of a Sun King" was dead on. Repeating a pattern that went all the way back to his days at Brébeuf, Trudeau kept a handful of men near him during his time in office whose influence over him was often pivotal. The balance of power had shifted, so that Trudeau was more father now than son, yet the same complex dynamic of a carefully circumscribed intensity often marked these relationships. James Coutts, for instance, who was Trudeau's principal secretary from 1975 to 1981, came to be seen as an almost Svengali-like figure for his ability to win Trudeau over to his stratagems and to successfully package the Trudeau image. It was Coutts who would engineer the defeat of the Conservative minority in 1979, and Coutts who would woo Trudeau out of retirement and lead him to victory in 1980. Yet, like Marc Lalonde and before him Jean Marchand, Coutts was never to develop a personal relationship with Trudeau; Trudeau saved that for his women. A strange kind of territoriality may have been playing itself out, then, between Margaret and people like Ivan Head, one in which the jealousy ran in both directions, each sensing that one controlled a sphere that was closed to the other.

None of this goes very far, however, toward explaining the public's fascination with the saga of Maggie and Pierre. Part of the fascination in Canada, of course, was the fascination itself: that the world's eyes should be upon us, that suddenly this backwater nation made the pages of *People* magazine and *Variety* and the British tabloids. Beyond that, their relationship seemed the logical completion of the Trudeau myth, embodying socially what Trudeau had seemed to embody politically. Youth, surely, which was a perpetual theme with him, but also the fairy-tale kingdom, the successful quest, the grail brought back that would restore the land. Like Trudeau's pirouette behind the Queen or his sandals in the House of Commons, which John Diefenbaker, epitome of the Old Guard, had muttered and fumed over, Maggie was a sign of the passing of the old order, the fusty colonial one of the Family Compact and the Union Jack.

It was uncanny how much the later story of Princess Di came to mirror that of Margaret Trudeau. Plucked from relative obscurity, married at twenty, the darling of the camera who, however, could not quite seem to get things right. Another fairy-tale marriage that went badly wrong—and for similar reasons. In the Canadian way, however, Maggie and Pierre ended rather less tragically and less bitterly. And while for England the tale of Charles and Di was more a matter of endings than beginning, the possible final chapter in the bloody, illustrious history of the British monarchy, for Canada, Maggie and Pierre were a beginning: at some level, and at long last, they were our own, homebred aristocracy. In matters of decorum Maggie was no match for the Queen, but the Queen was fond of her (something that couldn't quite be said for Diana), producing a hat pin when Maggie's hat blew off at their first meeting and showing Maggie how to fix her hat in place with it.

Margaret's comments about Trudeau's actresses and starlets were to hold truer for his post-Margaret era than they did for his pre-Margaret one. The old pattern of long-distance relationships was there, but it was much more conscious now. In some ways Trudeau truly became the playboy he had only feigned to be when he was younger, though the image never detracted from that of being a consummate father to his boys. As for his philandering, there would be many women who would attest to it, shocked to find a counterpart leaving by the back door as they came in through the front, but few who would abandon him for it. Women stayed in his life for years, well after relationships had ended; there might be bitternesses, but never ill wishes.

About Margaret's evening with the Rolling Stones Trudeau had said to interviewers, with what seemed real feeling, "I don't expect Margaret to stop going to rock concerts and to visit friends in New York because some people will be misled into thinking she's not behaving right. So, it's okay with me." In his last years, after the death of their youngest son, it was Margaret he most took solace from, and Margaret who sat at his bedside day and night as he died.

CHAPTER SEVEN

Notwithstanding

In some ways, the 1970s turned out much like the 1950s for Trudeau. A big bang at the beginning—the Asbestos Strike, the October Crisis—but then nothing much to show for all his hard work by the end. His fledgling attempts at putting in play his notion of "participatory democracy," the committees and white papers and weekend retreats, got bogged down in procedural issues and endless debate. His Just Society initiatives—in unemployment insurance, in regional development, in equalization programs—not only had dubious results but fed a national debt that rose from a mere $18 billion in 1968 to $100 billion by 1979, so that in eleven years Trudeau's Liberals accumulated four times as much debt as the preceding administrations had done since Confederation. The constitution, despite the conferences and tentative accords, was no closer to patriation than it had been in the fifty years of attempts by various governments, and Trudeau's cherished Charter of Rights and Freedoms remained a pipe dream. Meanwhile the one big initiative that Trudeau had pushed through, official bilingualism, had not even been his own, and had done nothing to stem the tide either of western alienation or of Quebec separatism. With the election of René Lévesque's Parti Québécois in 1976, separatism was actually at its height, with a referendum in the offing that despite all Trudeau's efforts at national reconciliation threatened shortly to split the country in two.

The one thing Trudeau could say was that despite the October Crisis and the Energy Crisis and stagflation and the spiralling debt, he had survived, even if just barely. He had won the shakiest of minorities in 1972 and then a majority in 1974 that he owed mainly to the boost Margaret had given his image on the campaign trail and to his spirited mockery of a Conservative proposal for wage and price controls—"Zap, you're frozen!"—over which he would have to eat crow not long after his re-election. But in May 1979, while Margaret seemingly danced on his grave at Studio 54, the magus who could not lose an election saw the Conservatives win a minority under leader Joe Clark, a man who had been known until then as Joe Who. When Trudeau announced his retirement shortly afterwards, he confirmed for many people what they had always suspected, in a charge that echoed the one levelled against him in the 1950s: that he was a dilettante, that he had entered politics as a diversion, losing interest in the game as soon as he no longer controlled it.

There has been much speculation about what Trudeau's legacy might have been had not Clark bungled a confidence vote six months into his term or had not Trudeau—after many exhortations, still playing the reluctant bride—agreed to return to lead the Liberals in the election that followed. Perhaps it would merely have been the legacy of most prime ministers, that of having been part of initiatives they didn't start and didn't finish, of having been eccentrics, in one way or another, of having done some things well and others poorly. Yet somehow, with Trudeau, the whole would have been greater than the sum of his parts. For the many people who followed Canadian politics merely as a kind of background static, who might normally have sooner tuned in to an American leadership debate than to a Canadian one, Trudeau had turned their heads, had made them think more of themselves, well before he had slain the dragon of referendum or brought home the constitutional grail.

But slay the dragon he did. If Trudeau's last term was his most officially triumphant one, however, and the culmination, really, of a lifetime of thinking and effort, it was also his most cynical and perhaps his most boring. By that time, spending, seemingly now through true indifference rather than as a matter of actual policy, had burgeoned out of control: in his last term alone Trudeau managed to double the debt, to $200 billion, leaving a legacy of interest costs that has hobbled every government that has followed him. Then there were the preferments and the patronage, including a spree of appointments as he was going out the door that completely doomed his hapless successor, the former golden boy John Turner. But at least he brought the constitution home, succeeding where many others had failed, and he managed to have enshrined in it, perhaps forever and for all time, his beloved Charter of Rights and Freedoms.

Trudeau had set the stage for his last, ultimately successful constitutional push the night before the 1980 Quebec referendum. Speaking to a capacity crowd in the Paul Sauvé Arena in Montreal, where four years earlier René Lévesque had celebrated the PQ election victory, he made clear that he had no intention of negotiating sovereignty association in the event of a "Yes" victory but promised to interpret a "No" as a mandate to begin at once the process of constitutional reform. In essence he turned the referendum on its head, portraying a "Yes" vote as a dead end and a "No" as a vote for change. Commentators would later say that his speech that night, one of only four Trudeau made during the referendum campaign, turned the tide of the referendum. That may have been the case, though it was clear at the time that he was speaking to the converted. Perhaps not so much converted to the "No" as converted to Trudeau: he was why people were there. On referendum night, it would be the loser, René Lévesque, whose hall would be packed to capacity, while the arena of the "No" side, presided over by the crotchety new provincial Liberal leader of the day, Claude Ryan, who had taken over from Bourassa, would stand half empty.

If Trudeau tilted the results—polls a week or so before had had the "Yes" side in the lead—he likely did so simply because he was Trudeau. Trudeau appeared very much the elder statesman at Paul Sauvé Arena, as if with the turn of the decade he had shed his old, gunslinger image. Yet, despite the frequent ovations and his own apparent emotion, there was a certain political hollowness to his speech, a certain posturing. If Quebecers took him at his word it was because by now he had grown truly iconic, a father figure to take direction from at a difficult turning, not so different from what his old nemesis Maurice Duplessis had once been. Claude Charron, Lévesque's point man during the referendum, later put it this way: "Lévesque is what we are, but Trudeau is what we would like to be."

Marshall McLuhan once identified the secret of Trudeau's charisma as his ability to look as if he contained many different people rather than a single lowly one. That night at the arena, thanks to the opening Lévesque had given him by his disparaging reference to Trudeau's "Elliott" side a few days earlier, Trudeau became the quintessential Canadian. In a rare moment, he vaunted his dual heritage, calling his name truly "*canadien,*" with a sense that reversed the old Quebec exclusivity of the term. Then he pointed to himself and said, "I ask you: is this the face of an exclusively European man?"—a reference to the frequent speculation about his own Aboriginal blood. Whatever rhetoric there might have been in the ploy, it was also as if he was facing the anonymous accuser back at Brébeuf who had suggested he would betray his race, but with an understanding now of the insidiousness of this type of racialist thinking.

Later, of course, Trudeau's promise in this speech to interpret a "No" as a vote for change would come back to haunt him. "But what change?" Lévesque said afterwards. "The sphinx kept his secret." Trudeau responded that everything was on the table, though by everything he didn't mean his Charter and he didn't mean federalism itself. What he meant, it began to grow clear as the first talks started, was more or less what he had meant ever since the first constitutional conference he had attended in 1950 as a junior clerk with the Privy Council. By now Trudeau was an old hand at constitutional discussions, which had been going on almost continuously since he'd taken office, and he had developed a fairly limited idea of what were acceptable compromises to his notion of federalism. He also knew that the broader the discussions grew, the harder it would be to reach any consensus. With a plump majority in Parliament and the mandate of the Quebec people for constitutional change, he sent his new constitutional bulldog, Jean Chrétien, across the country to work out a preliminary package with the provincial premiers.

If Trudeau had been the front man for the "No" victory, then Chrétien, *le p'tit gars de Shawinigan,* had been his enforcer. It had quickly grown clear that Claude Ryan, the Quebec Liberal leader but also Trudeau's old adversary as editor of *Le Devoir,* had had only a half-hearted commitment to the "No" side, putting forward tepid, abstract arguments and sulking at being seen as a puppet of the federalists. Chrétien had worked the province from end to end, replacing Ryan's abstractions with his from-the-heart straight talk and with many jibes at the condescending intellectualism of the Péquistes. Now he met with each of the premiers and got rough consensus from all but one,

Lévesque, who refused to meet with him. Everything fell apart, however, at the first joint conference: Lévesque showed up, but the Quebec delegation had got to the other premiers and undone all of Chrétien's legwork, getting them to sign on to a list of twenty-two concessions they wanted from the federal government before agreeing to patriation.

In his memoirs, Trudeau would maintain that it was already clear by then that Lévesque had no intention of letting the process succeed. "Listen, Jean, don't waste your time," one of Lévesque's ministers had apparently told Chrétien. "We are separatists. So we are not really interested in renewing Canada." The logic is hard to dispute. In the face of it, however, it had to be clear to Trudeau that the entire objective of this round of talks, that of rewarding the Quebecois for their "No," was doomed from the start. Why, then, did he press on? "What's the hurry, Prime Minister?" the premiers had said to him in the 1970s, a question repeated in a *Globe and Mail* editorial in 1980. Trudeau, of course, had an answer. In reference to the *Globe* editorial, he told Clarkson and McCall he was afraid that if the opportunity was missed this time, the country might not last long enough to get another one. "It would become a confederation of shopping centres," he said, a snipe at Joe Clark's view of Canada as a "community of communities," which to

Trudeau suggested a place without a centre, without a vision of itself. Whatever cynicism had come into Trudeau by then, he apparently still retained this unusual idealism about Canadian federalism, the sense that with a proper balance of powers for its governments and proper constitutional protections for its citizens it could achieve a kind of utopian state.

There had always been something of an American spirit to Trudeau, despite his affront at the charge back at Brébeuf. That had been his father's spirit, reinforced in Trudeau by trips to New York and his summers at Old Orchard, and especially by his stint at Harvard. Harvard had been his turning point, and after it, an American idealism had always lurked beneath his Canadian pragmatism, notable particularly in his ongoing commitment to a charter of rights and freedoms. Trudeau was never one to kowtow to the Americans, and he was soundly loathed by some of their presidents. "Asshole," Nixon had called him on one of his tapes, and Trudeau had responded, "I've been called worse things by better people." But nowhere was constitutionalism more a religion than in the United States. Trudeau was the man of bilingualism and of language rights, yet he knew that the ultimate function of a charter of rights was to shift a country's culture away from the commonalities of history and language and blood toward a commonality of values,

values that ultimately knew no borders. That made people citizens of the world. If Quebec nationalists saw a threat to their own notion of Quebecois culture in his vision, they were right to. However much a charter would protect the right to difference, it would ultimately be assimilationist in its emphasis on universality and on the individual, as the American model showed.

It would be hard to be sure, then, what promise Trudeau had imagined he was making to Quebecers at the Paul Sauvé Arena, much as René Lévesque afterwards suggested. In his memoirs, Trudeau said, "And the changes I was promising, were, of course, those we subsequently accomplished: bringing home our constitution, with a charter of rights and an amending formula." Such a claim, however, can't help but sound disingenuous. If he had offered these things from the stage—the very ones he had always been fighting for, Trudeau said in his defence, but also the ones Quebec had always rejected—the referendum would surely have been lost. In a documentary on the referendum, *Le confort et l'indifférence,* Denys Arcand replayed over and over that promise in the arena, juxtaposing it to subsequent events until it seemed the worst sort of snake-oil salesmanship. "Yet some people," Trudeau complained, adding they were "usually separatists," had "the gall" to charge "I led Quebeckers to believe that I would transfer all sorts of powers to Quebec and give it special status."

Whatever was driving Trudeau forward in the talks, then, it didn't seem to be a wish to appease the people of Quebec. Pure megalomania, some would later argue, the need for a legacy; or unbending idealism; or perhaps, again, the same paternalism he had derided in people like Duplessis, the sense that he knew best. As for Quebec, he must have hoped that no one there would notice his sleight of hand: he had played one thing off against the other, using the promise of constitutional talks to defeat the referendum and the referendum defeat to force the talks. Yet at the end of the day there would seem very little connection between the two matters.

TRUDEAU'S RESPONSE to the premiers' list of twenty-two demands was to put into action a threat he had been making since the mid-1970s, that of bypassing the provinces entirely and attempting to patriate the constitution on his own. He knew he had the support of Margaret Thatcher and of the Queen and that nothing in the law clearly prohibited the move. He announced his intention publicly in October 1980, presenting a patriation package that included his Charter. Immediately two premiers signalled their approval of the action, Bill Davis of Ontario and Richard Hatfield of New Brunswick. Both of them had been around at the last full-fledged constitutional conference in 1971, when a tentative agreement had fallen through after Quebec's Robert Bourassa had got cold feet.

The remaining eight provinces, however—the Gang of Eight, they came to be known as—were officially furious, though only one of them, Quebec, understood the true perfidy at work. With the unveiling of his package Trudeau had let the cat out of the bag, making clear that what he had meant by change was merely more of the same. In English Canada, the Trudeau stratagem was depicted as just one more chess move in the long game of federal–provincial negotiations, but in Quebec the sense of betrayal was palpable. The plan was "a revolting attempt to emasculate Quebec's history to better block its future," René Lévesque said, sounding almost too disgusted for words. But some of the people most furious were Trudeau's former allies in the referendum campaign. "Trudeau's screwed me," Claude Ryan fumed to anyone who would listen, an assessment verified when Lévesque called an election in spring 1981 and buried Ryan at the polls.

The Gang of Eight began a three-tiered attack to stymie Trudeau's plan for unilateral patriation, lobbying the British parliament to oppose him, putting together an alternative package that left out the Charter, and initiating a legal challenge that slowly wound its way to the Supreme Court of Canada. A year had passed since Trudeau had introduced his package by the time the court handed down a decision. The judges ruled, in a dog's breakfast of split decisions, that while Trudeau's move was not downright illegal, it was certainly not conventional, since convention in Canadian constitutional matters had normally required "substantial" provincial support. Having pronounced on convention, however, the court, to further complicate the issue, made clear it had no jurisdiction over convention, which was a matter for politicians.

Trudeau very briefly played the ruling as a victory, though apparently he had had an agreement all along with B.C. premier Bill Bennett to return to the table in the event of a mixed decision. Political scientist Peter Russell called the judgment "questionable jurisprudence" but "bold statecraft": by balancing the federal government's legal rights against the provinces' political ones, the court was essentially ensuring that the only prudent course for all parties was to return to the negotiating table. Trudeau's opponents were quick to point out that "convention" was not such a small matter in the Canadian system. The office of prime minister, for instance, was a matter of convention, as was another

major underpinning of Canadian democracy, the five-year
limit on a government's term in office. In any event, by the
time of the ruling Margaret Thatcher had already begun to
backtrack on the promise of easy patriation, after a slew of
provincial delegations had passed through London
denouncing Trudeau's plan.

In November 1981, Trudeau and the ten provincial premiers met at the old Ottawa train station, now converted to
the National Conference Centre, to try to hammer out a
deal. In the opening parry the Gang of Eight, ostensibly still
holding solid, presented their Charterless alternative package
as if it were a *fait accompli*. Trudeau would later claim that
the package clearly showed Lévesque was negotiating in bad
faith, since it contained an amending formula that gave up
the veto Quebec had traditionally considered non-negotiable.
Abandoning the constitutional veto amounted to accepting
the principle of provincial equality that had always been
anathema to Quebec nationalists. The compromise, in
Trudeau's view, could only mean Lévesque had no intention
of signing a deal and that his sole purpose was "to keep the
Gang of Eight intact to thwart me."

Clarkson and McCall, however, gave a different view in
Trudeau and Our Times. The new amending formula had
been cobbled together by the English members of the Gang

of Eight back while Lévesque had been busy with his election. Rather than a veto, it offered a clause that would allow Quebec—though also every other province—to opt out, with compensation, of national programs that encroached on provincial jurisdictions. According to Clarkson and McCall, Lévesque was pressured into flying to Ottawa for a late-night session with the other premiers just three days after his election victory, where he agreed to the new formula without having thought through its implications. It was not the first time Lévesque had made that sort of impulsive error, sometimes with grave consequences. The previous year, he made what might have been a fatal one with regard to the timing of the referendum. It had always been agreed within the party that a referendum campaign shouldn't overlap with a federal election, because people's loyalties would be divided; when Clark's Tories fell and Trudeau was suddenly crisscrossing the province again on the campaign trail and packing assembly halls, the assumption was that the referendum that had been set for that spring would be postponed. But when Claude Ryan rose up in Quebec's National Assembly to ask if the referendum would proceed as planned, Lévesque, to his party's horror, announced that it would. For the Parti Québécois, it was a first strike against their once-steadfast leader. His agreement to the new amending formula was a second one; the third was shortly to come.

Essentially, then, Trudeau was right in his analysis, even if for the wrong reasons: Lévesque could not sign an agreement that gave him no veto. Quebec thus went into the talks with its hands so severely tied that the talks' failure would have been practically the only acceptable outcome. For that outcome, however, Quebec was entirely dependent on the solidarity of the Gang of Eight. Lévesque had initially signed on with the group simply as a stratagem, to defeat what he called, using a term he knew would be especially laden for Trudeau, an "authoritarian" view of federalism. But the Supreme Court decision, which had made reference to the convention of "substantial" rather than unanimous provincial agreement, had in fact completely changed the rules of negotiation: no longer could Quebec play the spoiler against the rest, as it had in 1971. Even though the Supreme Court had claimed no jurisdiction in the area of convention, its ruling on the matter would prove crucial. Essentially it had argued that the veto Quebec had traditionally assumed, in fact, by "convention," didn't really exist.

The glue that bound the members of the Gang of Eight was their common resistance to Trudeau's Charter. They objected in general to the limitations a charter would place on provincial power by giving the courts a much broader say in many areas of provincial jurisdiction, and they objected specifically to some of the clauses that were especially dear to Trudeau, in particular the entrenchment of minority language rights. This was a hot-button issue in the West, where both anti-Trudeau and anti-French sentiment were running high at the time. But for Lévesque, the issue was a deal breaker. In Quebec, minority rights meant English rights. Entrenching minority language rights would have repercussions across a whole range of powers that Quebec saw as central to the defence of its culture, most notably the coveted *loi 101,* which under the Parti Québécois had firmly entrenched French as the province's sole official language and had ushered in a wide array of language reforms. Quebec nationalists had little faith in Trudeau's vision of a bilingual country, convinced their French-Canadian brethren outside Quebec were doomed to extinction. They had thus found themselves in the peculiar situation of having common cause with those anglophone provinces where bilingualism had become a symbol of federalist tyranny.

From the outset of the November negotiations, however, rifts began to appear in the coalition. Roy Romanow, the Attorney General of Saskatchewan and a born conciliator, was seen making asides to federal negotiator Jean Chrétien. An air of mutual distrust began to arise between the anglophone premiers and Lévesque, who felt that there was much more at stake for him than for the others and that issues that were central to Quebec were just a matter of horse-trading for the anglophones. Daniel Latouche, one of Lévesque's advisers, described the other premiers as "a bunch of Kiwanis presidents," ready to make a deal for a promise of money or a new factory. For two days the coalition held firm, but on the third day, in the suite at the Château Laurier where the Gang of Eight gathered every morning to discuss strategy, Saskatchewan premier Allan Blakeney presented a new compromise proposal that his people had obviously been working out for some time. It offered no veto for Quebec and no provision for opting out of federal programs. Lévesque was livid. It seemed the anglophones were trying to take away, bit by bit, everything that mattered to Quebec. The coalition was cracking.

Over the previous days, Trudeau had merely listened to the premiers' proposals and rejected them one by one. He would later say his strategy had been "to make a certain number of concessions" that would split the ranks of the Gang of Eight, but he had yet to offer any. Then on the third day, he declared that the talks were at an impasse. He had a proposal, however: that they bring the British North America Act home as it was, then put the premiers' constitutional package next to his own and let the public choose between the two in a referendum vote.

The idea was one he had borrowed from himself. Trudeau had always included a referendum clause of this sort in his own reform packages, as a way of allowing the public to break any future constitutional deadlocks. His strategy in proposing the idea now was spur of the moment, he later implied, yet he knew that the English premiers despised referendums, while the separatists were great promoters of them.

At the table, none of the anglophones took the bait. But then Trudeau, in his version of events, put the question to Lévesque during the coffee break.

"Surely a great democrat like yourself won't be against a referendum?" he said, no doubt a response to Lévesque's jibe about his "authoritarian" federalism. In Clarkson and McCall's account of the exchange, Trudeau went on to taunt Lévesque like a schoolyard bully. "You're the great believer in referendums. *You* can't be opposed to one.… Or are you afraid to take me on?"

As he had with Claude Ryan the year before, Lévesque, in Trudeau's words, "rose to the bait. I think he answered instinctively, without remembering that he was in the Gang of Eight, and said: 'Well, I can buy that.' I think he had in mind that this would be his chance to avenge his loss in the 1980 referendum, because I remember him saying, 'I would like to fight the charter.'"

It was Lévesque's third strike. He had broken the common front. Even his own team didn't realize at first what he had done, making jubilant phone calls back to Quebec City while Trudeau, who had either been lucky, or brilliant, or utterly Machiavellian, deadpanned to reporters: "We have a new alliance, between the Quebec government and the Canadian government." But then he added with a mischievous smile, "And the cat is among the pigeons."

Canadian history since then has rested, perhaps, on that single Lévesque gaffe. That afternoon, as the federal team began to suggest the terms of a referendum, which Lévesque said looked like they were "written in Chinese," it grew clear to the Quebec team that Lévesque had made a fatal misstep. The backroom negotiations started even before the premiers had broken for the day, up in a fifth-floor kitchen of the conference centre, where the *p'tit gars de Shawinigan* and the two Roys, Saskatchewan's Roy Romanow and Ontario Attorney General Roy McMurtry, were already cobbling together the first draft of what would come to be known as the Kitchen Accord. In fact, Chrétien and the Roys had been working out a counterdeal ever since the Supreme Court decision had come down, waiting for the moment to try to push it through. They got it when Lévesque unexpectedly broke ranks with the Gang of Eight.

Chrétien and his assistants worked through the night, making calls to the anglophone premiers at their Ottawa hotels and meeting with members of the provincial delegations in the Saskatchewan suite of the Château Laurier. By dint of trade-offs and concessions and tinkering with clauses and codicils, they managed by morning to bring on board all seven of the anglophone members of the Gang of Eight. Lévesque, meanwhile, staying over in Hull, was never called.

OF THE HEADS OF GOVERNMENT who ended up signing the accord on November 5, 1981, sixteen years to the day since Trudeau was first elected to Parliament, the last holdout was Trudeau himself. He would later do what he claimed never to do: express regret, seeming genuinely disappointed at some of the concessions he was talked into in the final hours of negotiation. It was in these frenzied late-night discussions that the infamous "notwithstanding" clause entered the agreement, as a swap for minority-language education rights. To Trudeau, the clause risked making his Charter into a farce. Meanwhile, the provision for a referendum in the event of a federal–provincial deadlock had been removed. Trudeau insisted he would rather return to his original plan of unilateral patriation and a referendum, even though one of his only two provincial allies, Richard Hatfield, had made clear he now opposed the idea.

Then late in the night Trudeau got a call from Bill Davis. If Trudeau passed up the deal, Davis said, he would be on his own. It was Davis who tipped the balance. Trudeau knew that with not a single province behind him, his chances at Westminster, in the face of the Supreme Court decision, would be extremely slim.

When news of the accord was made public, the tone in English Canada was one of cautious approval. A CBC report that followed the signing had a celebratory air, with the fact of Lévesque's exclusion tacked on toward the end, as if it were merely a sad but predictable footnote. "Once again," Lévesque said, "Quebec is where it always has been, alone," coming across a bit like Malvolio shaking his fist and vowing revenge amidst the general merriment at the end of *Twelfth Night*. The news report raised no question of Trudeau's promise at the Paul Sauvé Arena or of how an accord that actually reduced Quebec's powers could constitute a fulfillment of it. And while Trudeau expressed sadness that Quebec had not signed and he promised to work "in the coming weeks" to bring Quebec into the final package, he didn't, on this matter, express regret.

The tone of approval in English Canada had much to do with the fact that Trudeau the Intransigent had finally, like a good Canadian, made some concessions. An editorial in *The Globe and Mail* called the deal "A set of compromises in the true Canadian tradition. Every first minister has given up something dear to him. Mr. Trudeau has given up much." But then the piece went on, somewhat astoundingly, to praise Trudeau for burying the French question.

> Perhaps most important, he has diminished the importance of Mr. Levesque's [sic] opposition, by being himself a French-Canadian Prime Minister, who had more Quebeckers behind him in his last election than had Mr. Levesque [sic]. This fight was not, though Mr. Levesque [sic] strove to present it as such, a French-English fight.

The comment was typical not only of the flawed understanding of Quebec politics in English Canada—the facts suggested that Quebecers had re-elected Lévesque exactly because they wanted him at the constitutional table—but of the general feeling that Lévesque had merely got what he deserved. Again, Trudeau's promise of change had been forgotten. For most English Canadians, in fact, the fine print of the deal was of little interest. What seemed more important at the time was less the substance of the deal than its symbolism: after a hundred and fourteen years, Canada, at last, had brought the constitution home. Back at the failed Victoria Conference of 1971, Trudeau had bemoaned what he said was "the last remnant of a condition that is not worthy of Canada as a free and independent country," namely that it could not amend its own constitution. He had changed that. He had pulled the sword from the stone. Many Canadians must have wondered why it had taken so long.

In Quebec, of course, as with most things, the accord played differently. Chrétien's night of "horse-trading" would come to be referred to, without apparent irony, as "The Night of the Long Knives," a reference to Hitler's famous purge of his political enemies.

"Every one of them hated the goddamn son of a bitch," Lévesque said afterwards of the other premiers. "For their own particular reasons. But none of them had a vision of politics that couldn't be turned by a couple of cocktails."

Eventually, the constitutional accord would take its place next to the October Crisis as one of the great perfidies committed against the Quebec people by the traitor Trudeau. In the case of the accord, however, the charge had much greater cause. Lévesque had had a mandate from Quebecers to negotiate change, to hold Trudeau to his promise, and Trudeau had run roughshod over it. In agreeing to an accord that reduced Quebec's powers, whether he did so out of expedience or pure desperation, he had betrayed his promise of 1980. Trudeau afterwards played with the numbers to suggest, as the *Globe* editorial had, that the federal Liberals' strength in Quebec constituted support for the accord, but the success of the separatist Bloc Québécois in later years was surely fed by Quebecers' lingering sense of betrayal over the constitution and their loss of trust in their federal representatives. While it was the breakaway Conservative Lucien Bouchard who formed the Bloc in a split with Brian Mulroney over Meech Lake, it would be the federal Liberals who would most feel the effects, being no longer able to rely comfortably on their Quebec base.

In the immediate aftermath of the talks, however, Lévesque took it on the nose in Quebec as much as he did in the rest of Canada. Claude Ryan raked him over the coals in the National Assembly, saying that far from being the victim of "diabolical machinations" among the anglophone premiers, he had been done in by "the hopeless contradiction of a provincial sovereignist negotiating for renewed federalism." Meanwhile, his own party was pressing him for either a new election or a new referendum. "Il m'a fourré," Lévesque had said in tears on the plane back to Quebec, just as Ryan had said before him. He screwed me. But no one got points for being outwitted. Two native sons, two titans, had clashed, and Trudeau had come out the winner. Lévesque was never to recover.

"If Trudeau had become a separatist in the 60s," journalist Denise Bombardier remarked, "Quebec would be independent by now."

Of course, Trudeau was Trudeau because he hadn't. It was the one time, perhaps, that he had truly gone against the current, almost alone among his set in bucking the nationalist trend of the Quiet Revolution. It was not an easy turning, leading not only to lifelong rifts with people like his old mentor and friend from Brébeuf, François Hertel, but to a feeling of betrayal among a younger generation who had been looking to him as their hero and who, as Quebec journalist Malcolm Reid observed, could not forgive him the "cool, assured tone" with which he distanced himself from their fiery nationalism. "How could he live in the smothering of liberty and not cry, not scream, not scribble on walls, not take to drink or dynamite?" But he had already been there and found it a dead end; it was exactly what had given birth to the "functional politics" he had announced in the first issue of *Cité libre* and had stuck to ever since.

However cynical Trudeau became by the final years, and however much he played off his promises to achieve his own ends, there was a continuity, at least, in his vision. In *Federalism and the French Canadians,* he had reached the conclusion that "federalism has all along been a product of reason in politics. It was born of a decision by pragmatic politicians to face facts as they are, particularly by the fact of the heterogeneity of the world's population. It is an attempt to find a rational compromise between the divergent interest-groups which history has thrown together; but it is a compromise based on the will of the people." This had always remained for him the appeal of federalism, that it based itself not on ethnicity and emotionalism but on practicality and the common good. Trudeau may have come to this stance by way of the cauldron of his own crises of identity, but the reason he stuck with it was because it made sense. And if he had patched it together via Harvard and Harold Laski and China and the Khyber Pass, it was, in the end, a very Canadian stance.

Historian Michael Bliss, in his article "Guarding a Most Famous Stream," has made the argument that far from being the political maverick he was often portrayed as, Trudeau followed very much in the traditions of the prime ministers who had preceded him. "Pierre Trudeau was undeniably more abrasive, arrogant, tough, aloof, solitary, and self-contained than traditional politicians," he says, and

> brought to the prime ministership intellectual skills, life experiences, and values different from those brought by most of his predecessors. Once in office, however, he was not as unlike them as even his own ornery reflections imply. He brokered competing interests, bought political support, and doled out patronage in the grand Canadian manner. He stood firmly on guard for Canada when it was menaced. He greatly expanded the freedoms of Canadians. In these regards he was a true inheritor of the mantles of William Lyon Mackenzie, Sir John A. Macdonald, Wilfred Laurier, William Lyon Mackenzie King, Lester Pearson, even John Diefenbaker. Some maverick.

Just as he had done when he was a student at Brébeuf, Trudeau had found the way in politics to marry the stance of the rebel to the slog of getting on with the job. "The truth is I work." It was such a quintessentially Canadian sentiment, as true of the *habitant* stock of New France and the Scots Presbyterians and Irish refugees of Upper Canada as of the First Nations running their traplines and the latter-day immigrants of every hue. Perhaps our attraction to him came exactly from this, that however different from us he seemed, however much the outsider, we sensed he was one of us. He gave the impression of adventure and change even as he affirmed the general flow of things as they were. Rebellion without risk. A very Canadian sort of rebellion. Or put differently: he showed us how to be ourselves, but to do it with style.

CHAPTER EIGHT

He Haunts Us Still

In the mid-1980s, I did graduate studies in Montreal with the vague intention of making myself a better, more bilingual Canadian. If I became a better Canadian, however, it was probably less from my immersion in our other official culture, which felt much more remarkably foreign than I had expected, than from my tuning in to Peter Gzowski's *Morningside* every day while I had my breakfast. My apartment was near the downtown non-campus of Concordia University, and every day for nearly two years I would walk up one of the side streets north of Sherbrooke that had formed part of the old Golden Square Mile of the city's long-gone Scots elite to an outbuilding of Montreal General where I met with a Freudian analyst, as Trudeau himself had once done in Paris.

I didn't know about Trudeau's analysis then, though I knew that at his retirement he had purchased a house on Pine Avenue not two hundred paces from the little path that led up the slope of Mount Royal to my analyst's outbuilding.

He had paid $200,000 for it, the papers had said, which seemed a respectable sum at the time for someone of his eminence and means. When I finally dared to sneak a glance at the house, however, I was surprised at how unimpressive it looked, a tiny, boxlike place that clung to its narrow lot on that busy stretch of Pine without the least flourish or marker to set it apart. Later I would learn it had been built by Ernest Cormier, the designer of the Supreme Court building in Ottawa, and that it was considered an art deco masterpiece. At the time, however, I thought Trudeau had gone a bit far with his legendary frugality and might at least have sprung for a proper front lawn.

Every day as I trudged up the foothills of Mount Royal to my session, and particularly as I trudged down again and my back was to him, I thought of Trudeau perched in his little fortress on Pine Avenue. I had no particular desire to run into him, fearing, perhaps, that something would be lost then: he would prove truly as short as people said, or would snub me, or pick his nose. Yet it was Trudeau, perhaps single-handedly, who had brought me to Montreal. I had dutifully taken French all through high school and had even learned some; I had gone to Winter Carnival; I had done a month of intensive French at the Alliance Française in Paris. I had chosen Montreal for my graduate studies not because of the schools, of which I knew almost nothing, but for one reason only: the French. Who but Trudeau could I blame for this? He may not have invented bilingualism, but he had made it sexy; he might never have uttered the phrase "two solitudes," yet it was surely because of him that I felt obliged to break them down.

By the time I left Montreal in 1988, it would have been fair to say that my experiment in national reconciliation had been a resounding failure. By then I had come to realize that I was indeed what had seemed to have been stamped in my passport when I'd first arrived, an anglophone, and that the hard work of building cultural bridges, in Montreal as elsewhere, was exactly that, hard work. Who had the time, really? Between classes and coursework and psychoanalysis and worrying about datelessness and the state of the world, there weren't many hours left in the day for nation building. At Concordia, at least in the English department, the two solitudes still reigned—in two years of classes I met a single francophone Quebecer, around whom an aura of suspicion hung because he had thrown in his lot with the anglos when everyone knew the real action was in the other camp. Meanwhile a joint lecture series on literary theory that Concordia had organized with the Université du Québec à Montréal had deteriorated into a bit of a farce: in the search for a "neutral" location, the organizers had chosen a venue out near the old Expo site that required three bus transfers from downtown and a call ahead to the security guard to warn him you'd be coming. The lectures alternated between English and French; the francophones went to the French ones, and the anglophones to the English.

My own French, I quickly discovered, was not quite at the level that made conversing with me in it really worth the bother. It was just as well, as most of the francophones I ran into in the course of a day also spoke English, a language I was quite fluent in. In the four years I spent in Montreal, less French crossed my lips than in the single month I had spent at the Alliance Française in Paris. I had no one to blame for this except myself, though perhaps in a slightly less laden atmosphere—Togo, say, or Martinique—I have might been more willing to risk humiliation. It could have been that I simply never built up a sufficient escape velocity to cross over, to leave the familiar. But the more time that passed, the easier it became to stay in my little world, so that what had seemed incredible to me when I arrived, that there were people who had lived in Montreal all of their lives who didn't speak a word of French, made perfect sense to me when I left. Some years later I spent several days entirely immersed in francophone Montreal promoting the French translation of one of my novels, and I felt as if I had entered a completely different city than the one I had lived in for four years.

TO WHAT EXTENT, then, had Trudeau's vision succeeded? To judge from my own experience, not much. When I arrived in Montreal in 1984, it was true, the word on the street was that nationalism, for lack of interest, had died a quiet death: after the failed referendum and then the failed constitution, people had turned their attention to other matters. The young were more interested in finding jobs than in planning revolutions, and they were enrolling en masse in ESL courses to make up for their forced education in French under Bill 101. Meanwhile there was talk of a "victory of the cradle" much different from the one Quebec's Catholic Church had promoted earlier in the century. From having had one of the highest birth rates in the world then, Quebecers now had one of the lowest, so that soon the immigrant population would so have shifted the Quebec demographic that any hope of a successful referendum would have vanished.

By the time of my departure, however, the atmosphere in the city had completely changed. Out of nowhere, it seemed, crowds numbering in the tens of thousands were suddenly marching in the streets, as nationalist sentiment reared its hydra head again. If there was a single culprit to blame for the resurgence it was the mandarin on the hill, well into retirement now: Citizen Trudeau. Under the provisions of his Charter, the Quebec Court of Appeal had ruled unconstitutional the section of Bill 101 prohibiting English signs. All over the city, placards went up on people's balconies. *"Ne touchez pas à la loi 101!"* Hands off Bill 101. Suddenly all the old sentiment was there, all the sense of outrage. Robert Bourassa was back in office by then, after the demotion of Claude Ryan and the implosion of the PQ, and when the Supreme Court of Canada upheld the ruling of the Court of Appeal, Bourassa pulled out his nationalist colours to assure the public that the law would stand. Stand it did, as Bill 178, this time bearing the proud imprimatur of the Charter's "notwithstanding" clause. This was not the first time the clause had been invoked: René Lévesque, after the constitution had been passed into law, had bitterly attached it to every piece of legislation that had crossed his desk before he left office in 1985. But Bill 178 was the first use of the clause in specific response to a court ruling.

What had briefly felt like an end, then, turned out to be the merest lull. Over the next years it would seem that all of Trudeau's work had been for naught, that it had merely sown the seeds for another vicious cycle of polarization between

English and French. From the Charter came the challenge to 101; from the challenge came all the old nationalist bitterness; from the bitterness came the disastrous 1987 Meech Lake Accord of Progressive Conservative Prime Minister Brian Mulroney. While the accord was a perfectly legitimate attempt to do what Trudeau in 1981 had promised to do "in the coming weeks" but had never got around to, namely to find a way to bring Quebec into the constitution, it ended up fanning the flames of nationalist sentiment rather than putting them out, reopening the constitutional "can of worms" that Trudeau had claimed to have closed definitively. The accord's three-year timeline for ratification, required because it changed the constitution's amending formula, made it a sitting duck, providing ample opportunity for opposition to fester and grow against controversial clauses such as the one recognizing Quebec as a "distinct society."

When the accord failed, however, once again the fingers pointed to the man on the hill. As he had done at the Paul Sauvé Arena, Trudeau had intervened at the crucial moment, publishing an open letter in the *Toronto Star* and Montreal's *La Presse* bemoaning that the federation "set to last a thousand years"—an odd allusion to Hitler's thousand-year Reich that he later assured Peter Gzowski he had meant ironically—had not foreseen "that one day the government of Canada would fall into the hands of a weakling." Mulroney, Trudeau claimed, had "sold out" to the provinces and to the "snivellers"—read Premier Bourassa—from Quebec. The man whom his son Justin would praise at his funeral for teaching him never to attack the person, only the idea, was clearly willing in this case to break his own precepts. But then, point by point, he dissected the accord, painting a picture of a Canada where the federal government had become a mere tax collector, doling out everything it received to the provinces to spend as they saw fit. It was everything Trudeau had fought against. A confederation of shopping centres.

Before Trudeau weighed in, the accord had unanimous approval from the provinces, near-unanimous approval among the federal parties, and substantial approval among the general public, particularly in Quebec, where politicians and citizens alike had been especially pleased with the long-coveted special status Trudeau had always opposed. Afterwards, however, things began to fall apart. In extensive testimony before the Senate and the House, speaking without text, Trudeau made the argument against the accord, bringing to bear the full powers of his "legalistic" mind. "I think we have to realize that Canada is not immortal," he ended, "but, if it is going to go, let it go with a bang rather than a whimper." Meanwhile Canadians, heady with their new post-Charter rights, began to wonder aloud how issues of such fundamental importance had come to be decided by eleven overfed white men meeting behind closed doors at a lakeside retreat. As opposition mounted, however, so did the old tensions. A handful of anti-French incidents in the anglophone provinces received wide play in Quebec, so that any opposition to Meech came to be cast as the rejection, once again, of Quebec's aspirations. An infamous trampling of the fleur-de-lys in Brockville had a life that stretched over many months in the Quebec media, even though it had been a protest not against Meech but against provincial downloading of the costs of bilingualism.

Governments had come and gone by the time of the deadline for ratification. By then the "distinct society" clause had been so watered-down by amendments that Lucien Bouchard had left the Conservatives to form the Bloc and Robert Bourassa, not for the first time, had begun to waver. But the accord's initial, albeit symbolic defeat, had nothing to do with English or French: it came when First Nations MPP Elijah Harper raised an eagle feather in the Manitoba legislature to dissent on a vote to bypass public consultations that had required unanimity. Harper felt that the First Nations had not been properly consulted in the accord process.

Though a legal route was later found to get around the impasse in Manitoba, Newfoundland premier Clyde Wells killed the accord definitively when he refused to bring it to a vote in his legislature. Once again, Trudeau had won. In a rough equivalent of Lévesque's "Il m'a fourré," Mulroney would still be fulminating against Trudeau years after Trudeau was in the grave, pulling no punches against him in his memoirs and calling the demise of Meech "a death in the family" that had left him with "a throbbing sense of loss for one of the greatest might-have-beens in Canada's 140 year history." The blood had hardly dried over his Meech defeat, however, before Mulroney was back at the table again pounding out the Charlottetown Accord, a super-Meech that included public consultations and a grab-bag of new entice- ments, including strengthened Aboriginal rights, a triple-E Senate—equal, elected, and effective—and a "Canada clause" that said, in essence that, while Quebec was special, the "Rest of Canada," as it had now come to be known, was special too. From La Maison du Egg Roll in Montreal, one of his favourite haunts, Trudeau pronounced on Charlottetown: "This Mess Deserves a No." In the referendum that followed, Canadians took his advice and voted "No."

The decisive "No" vote in both English Canada and Quebec, however, was read less as a sign of a growing solidarity than of a widening gap. The accord covered such a wide range of issues that it provided almost everyone with something to object to. Yet thanks to a vocal minority in each of the solitudes—led by Preston Manning's fledgling Reform Party in English Canada and by the PQ and the Bloc in Quebec—the issue of too little or too much for Quebec was the one that lingered. Despite Trudeau's Herculean efforts at holding the country together, it seemed that Canada, as Lord Durham had put it back in 1838, was still "two nations warring within the bosom of a single state." In the 1995 Quebec referendum that the Charlottetown Accord had been a desperate attempt to avert, the war came within a hair's breadth of splitting the country, a single percentage point separating the "No" from the "Yes." The "No" forces had been led by Prime Minister Jean Chrétien, as despised by Quebec nationalists as Trudeau had ever been but not nearly as respected. Chrétien, in a move that may nearly have cost him the country, had specifically asked Trudeau to keep silent during the campaign.

On the twentieth anniversary of the Constitution Act of 1982, when Trudeau himself had already been dead a year and a half, every party leader in Quebec's National Assembly, including the former federalist Jean Charest, stood up in the Legislature to roundly denounce, in no uncertain terms, Trudeau's constitution. For those who back in 1968 had imagined on the one hand that here, finally, was a man to make a place for Quebec, or on the other that here was a man to put Quebec in its place, it could surely only seem that the Trudeau experiment had been a flop.

Federally, in the post-Trudeau era, the political landscape has become hopelessly balkanized, with no party able, or in some cases willing, to claim anything like a national mandate. Separatism has not died, but rather has become virtually a national institution, so that it is hard to remember how the country ever got along without it. Westerners continue to loathe the East, guarding their old grievances and always ready to add new ones. This, then, is the post-Trudeau One Canada. Meanwhile, despite the exchange programs and the immersion programs and the French and English on our cereal boxes, the level of bilingualism, according to Census Canada, rose a paltry 5 percent between 1961 and 2001, from 12 to 17 percent. Even those numbers are deceptive, skewed as they are by Quebec, the one province where bilingualism is actively discouraged, but where it runs at an alarming 40 percent; in the "Rest of Canada," it has stagnated at 10 percent.

Depending on how all these data are interpreted, the country is either going to hell in a handbasket or is humming along more or less as it always has. The Liberals have never done well in the West, nor the Conservatives in the East, and many regional parties have come and gone. Since Confederation more than a dozen parties have elected members to the House of Commons, including the Ralliement créditistes, a separatist-leaning Quebec splinter party that under Réal Caouette elected nine members in 1965 and fourteen in 1968. And while Calgary will likely never become meaningfully bilingual, or Toronto, despite the legions of parents sending their children into French immersion programs, Ottawa has become so, a situation that would have been unthinkable in the Ottawa Trudeau arrived at in 1950, as has Montreal, and as have Moncton and Sudbury.

The jury, then, is still out. This much is true: so far, the country has held. It continues to function, in fact, much as Trudeau envisioned, as a struggle among competing powers with competing interests that somehow works to the benefit of the people. The Canadian population has always understood federalism, tending to play its provincial governments against its federal ones. This is another of the contradictions that somehow found its still point in Trudeau: that what has held the country together has been exactly the forces that have always seemed on the verge of tearing it apart. Perhaps, going right back to the Conquest, when the British began almost at once to buy the compliance of the French Canadians with rights and privileges, English Canada has always needed a Quebec to appease, just as Quebec, in the way of all minorities, has always needed an English Canada to rail against to keep itself strong.

In the end it may simply have been the case that Trudeau's individualist vision was fundamentally incompatible with the more collectivist one of many of his fellow Quebecers. Yet the Quebec he left behind at his death was more or less the Quebec he had fought for: economically solvent, politically left-leaning, and with one of the highest standards of living in the world. It was a place utterly transformed from the Quebec of his childhood and from the years of *la Grande noirceur* of Duplessis. From the closed, puritan society of his youth Quebec had become practically its opposite—secular, cosmopolitan, progressive, vibrantly democratic. Moreover, it had managed to sustain the strength of the French language and had experienced a flourishing of culture that made it a model of innovation and cultural self-sufficiency. All this it had achieved without special powers or special status, without so much as even having signed the constitution, within the uncomfortable but familiar straitjacket of the Canadian federation. In 1993, after criticism from the United Nations Human Rights Committee, it even quietly dropped the "notwithstanding" clause from its language legislation and found the way to bring it within conformance of the Charter.

Once again, Trudeau had won.

A FEW YEARS AGO, on a return visit to Montreal, I took a commemorative stroll past Trudeau's house. A CBC crew was there, interested not in Trudeau, by then dead, but in the Cuban Consulate across the street. Back in my day the place had been decked out like a Hells Angels clubhouse, festooned with security cameras and barbed wire owing to a spate of firebombings by anti-Fidelistas, but now—a sign of the times—it was undergoing a condo conversion. I had never quite known what to make of Trudeau's chumminess with the Cubans. His little tête-à-tête with Fidel Castro at Cayo Largo had always seemed the political equivalent of Margaret's night with the Rolling Stones. Was it pure showmanship? A snub at the Americans? Yet in this, too, Trudeau was following in a Canadian tradition that went back to John A. Macdonald, who knew that snubbing the Americans was the surest way to gain credibility with Canadians. Trudeau claimed at the time that he was merely continuing a diplomatic relationship begun by John

Diefenbaker, which was in fact the case—Diefenbaker had defied both Eisenhower and Kennedy to maintain relations with Cuba after the Castro takeover. As questionable as the visit seemed, Trudeau was at least consistent: he had scooped Nixon in 1970 in recognizing Red China, and he brought a level of sensitivity to Soviet relations that ran completely counter to the Cold War logic of the Americans, which he had always despised.

Trudeau had visited each of these places before he entered politics: China in 1949 and again a decade later with Jacques Hébert, the Soviet Union for an economic conference in 1952, and Cuba in 1949 to cut sugarcane.

While I stood outside Trudeau's house watching the CBC crew, a woman with a lapdog came up to me.

"Did you know him?" she asked.

"No, no." I felt slightly ashamed at this. "I never met him."

"We used to have coffee sometimes. As friends. I met him in an elevator once and he invited me for dinner, and then we stayed friends."

A feeling of unreality came over me. There seemed something delusional in such a casual reference to the man, as if he were merely a local eccentric to talk fondly of, now that he'd gone. With a start, I realized what had been omitted in the comma between "invited me for dinner" and "then we stayed friends." So she had been a conquest.

"He was very gentle, you know. Very funny. Of course, if he gave you supper the portions were always very small."

The woman mentioned in passing—could this have been true?—that one of Pierre's neighbours had been none other than René Lévesque. She showed me the building up the street where he had had a condo, before he'd moved out to Nuns' Island.

Did they run into each other? Did they get along?

"Oh, you know, they were old friends since the 1950s. All the rest, it was just politics."

It hadn't looked like just politics at the time.

Across the way the CBC crew was still checking camera angles on the old Cuban Consulate. It seemed they had missed the real story.

"I still feel sad sometimes," the woman said. "That he's gone."

AN ARROGANT S.O.B. That was the assessment one often heard during his political years, as the stories were retold. Trudeau giving the finger to protesters in Salmon Arm. Saying to the grain farmers in Saskatchewan, "Why should I sell your wheat?" Shoving the National Energy Program down the throats of Albertans. Here is Robert Mason Lee's take on the NEP: "Did the eastern bastards, at the end of the day, ever freeze to death in the dark? Did the Alberta oil taps remain closed? Did the US industry forever abandon Alberta's sedimentary basin? Did the 'Canada lands' ever turn an honest dime? Do we now have Canadian control over the oil industry? Are our resources protected from the cupidity and avarice of the world markets? Of course not. Everything about the NEP as a policy instrument was ephemeral and illusory, but this much was real: My house dropped in value by one third overnight; my brother lost his job; my father, who had put his money into real estate at Uncle Allen's urging, saw his last chance of a comfortable retirement fly away like cinders. Whatever other objectives it might have claimed, the NEP was cruelly efficient at economic assassination."

A Keynesian idea whose time had gone. It may be some years, still, before the Liberals can rebuild in Alberta.

Trudeau was not always tactful, that much was true. In his final campaign, in 1980, his handlers were careful to keep him away from crowds because of his colourful ways with hecklers. But back in Salmon Arm, he would have said, they had deserved it: they were waving anti-French placards. And in Saskatchewan, with those farmers, the question had really been a Brébeufian rhetorical flourish, part of an argument about the importance of marketing boards. The farmers of Saskatchewan, however, had apparently not been in the mood for rhetorical flourishes.

No one who knew Trudeau personally would ever have thought to describe him as arrogant. He was too shy to be prime minister, his old Brébeuf friend and rival Jean de Grandpré had told him. And people who knew him outside of politics knew him as humble, as generous, as thoughtful, as warm. An attentive lover. A loyal friend. A loving father. After his retirement, his children became the focus of his life. If he had not found a lasting love with a woman, at least he had found it with them.

He had re-emerged into public life only twice after his retirement, both times decisively, to slay the monster of Meech and then the Son of Meech, Charlottetown. But the true monster he would fight, like Beowulf suiting up in old age to fight the unnamed dragon, would be the death of his son Michel, killed skiing in the Rockies in November 1998, when an avalanche swept him into Kokanee Lake. He was twenty-three.

In the hero tales, there is always something to pay. The infidelity of Guinevere. Odysseus's long journey home. Beowulf, mortally wounded, dies. It might have crossed

Trudeau's mind that Michel on the mountain, just as Trudeau himself had often done, had been pretending to be his father.

I COULD NOT QUITE FATHOM, back in the 1980s, what Trudeau's concern with the Charter was. I had assumed, in a general way, that we were already covered, and in fact we were. John Diefenbaker, of all people, had passed a Bill of Rights into law in 1961, and though the BNA Act overrode it, there were surely enough precedents in British common law, going all the way back to the Magna Carta and before, to cover most contingencies.

But I had misunderstood. For a precedent there is always a counter-precedent; not so with a charter. There is only one. Below it, every law of the land, every by-law, every precedent; above it, only sky. The Charter, legal experts say, has revolutionized the legal and political landscape. Just as Trudeau envisioned, the power has passed from the hands of the politicians, who now must meet the standards of the Charter with every bill. Whether the power has truly passed into the hands of the people or simply into those of the legal establishment is an unanswered question, though for many people the Charter, across a wide range of issues, has given rise to the same sort of national pride that Trudeau himself once aroused.

Not so much in Quebec, perhaps. In Quebec, the Charter has often been seen as merely the last stage in an erosion that went back to Trudeau's first days in office, when what had started out under Lester Pearson as a commission on biculturalism got reduced under Trudeau to one on mere bilingualism. In place of the bicultural country, Trudeau gave us the multicultural one, a move that in English Canada was often seen as a cynical ploy to woo the ethnic vote and in Quebec as another attempt to divide and conquer. For Trudeau, however, the notion of multiculturalism, however much Made in Canada it seemed, likely went back to the tag he had pinned to his door at Harvard, "Citizen of the World," when for the first time, perhaps, he had begun to understand politics in terms that went beyond his own narrow history and culture. That sudden opening of perspective would remain at the heart of his political vision, and of his notion of government not as the guardian of some sort of nationalistic ideal but as a practical attempt "to find a rational compromise between the divergent interest-groups which history has thrown together." This was a task as necessary in China, with its myriad ethnic groups, or in Africa, with its arbitrary colonial borders, as it was in Canada or as it would be in the former satellites of the Soviet Union. The Charter was Trudeau's attempt to encode this spirit of "rational compromise" in law so that the many could never trample the rights of the few.

The Charter was also, clearly, his swipe at the ethnic nationalism he saw still lurking in the separatist movement. In this, however, he ran up against a contradiction. While the Charter seems fundamentally incompatible with any notion of "special status" that bases itself on shared history or shared ethnicity, the idea of "many" and "few" grows ambiguous in the case of Quebec, where the francophone majority will always remain an embattled minority within the anglophone sea that surrounds it. There has also been a development in Quebec Trudeau might not have considered, the birth of a new sovereignist party, Quebec Solidaire, that disclaims any ties to ethnic nationalism, and that in 2008 sent its first MNA, Amir Khadir, to the Quebec National Assembly. Ironically, it is a party that Trudeau himself might have founded. In place of the appeal to shared history or shared blood, it appeals to exactly the sorts of shared values—pluralism, feminism, environmentalism—that have become the clarion call of the post-Charter generation.

A few years ago, not long after the Ontario Court of Appeal upheld a Charter challenge against Canadian marriage law, I served as one of the best men at the same-sex marriage of two friends at Toronto's City Hall. The first act of my friends as a newly and legally married couple was to serve as the witnesses for the couple who came in behind them. They had come from Quebec, where the same-sex challenge had not yet wound its way through the courts. It would be hard to imagine a stranger pairing: one was a rail-thin, blue-eyed Russian from Siberia who stood six-foot-seven and spoke not a word of English and only a smattering of French; the other was a pudgy Haitian from Port-au-Prince who stood maybe five feet in heels. Konstantin and Widy. They had driven five hours that morning from Montreal to say their vows—and would drive five hours back immediately afterwards to a waiting reception. They were clearly in love.

Back during the 1968 leaders' debate, Réal Caouette, leader of the Ralliement créditistes, joked that Trudeau's Criminal Code amendments might lead to a situation where "a man, a mature man, could in the future marry another mature man." Caouette had his joke while Trudeau, awaiting his response time, smiled civilly and held his tongue. In 1968 what Caouette was proposing was so far from the realm of the imaginable that it constituted a *reductio ad absurdum,* a rhetorical device Trudeau would have recognized from his Brébeuf days. In his response, Trudeau passed over the rhetoric and stuck to the substance, with impeccable logic, making Caouette's views seem suddenly a thing of the past.

Trudeau himself surely could not have envisioned back then, any more than Caouette could have, the scene I was part of in that city hall reception room. Yet in a real sense, he was responsible for it. Nearly forty years further on, I still felt his shadow at my back.

TRUDEAU DIED ON SEPTEMBER 28, 2000, a month short of his eighty-first birthday. Arrangements had been made for him to lie in state in Ottawa, then to be taken by train to Montreal to lie at City Hall before a funeral at Notre Dame Basilica. Organizers were unsure what the public's response would be to the death of someone who had left public life more than sixteen years earlier. They had their answer. One of them wrote:

> From the long lines on Parliament Hill, to the school children lining the tracks in Eastern Ontario and Western Quebec, to the crowds that met his casket when it arrived in Montreal, to the line-up to say goodbye at City Hall, to those who stood patiently outside the Cathedral during the funeral service, and finally, to the millions of Canadians who followed the events across the

country on television, the response was dignified, emotional, and massive.

He had been hated and loved, but mostly respected. At his eightieth birthday, his son Alexandre, in a rare interview, had talked of the lesson his father had learned from the Jesuits.

"You take what you are and you thrust it out as hard as you can. And what's left is what's true."

Trudeau was buried in the little town of Saint-Rémi-de-Napierville, his family's ancestral home. He had wanted to run there instead of in Mount Royal when he joined the Liberals in 1965, but Marchand had told him he couldn't win. Now, however, the town was happy to have him.

Annau, Catherine, dir. & wr. Documentary. *Just Watch Me: Trudeau and the 70s Generation* (National Film Board of Canada, 1999).

Borins, Sara, et al., eds. *Trudeau Albums.* (Toronto: Penguin, 2000).

Brittain, Donald, dir. & wr. Documentary. *The Final Battle: 1977–1985.* (National Film Board of Canada/Canadian Broadcasting Corporation, 1994).

Canadian Broadcasting Corporation. *CBC Digital Archives.* Available at: http://archives.cbc.ca/search?x=1&q=Pierre+trudeau &RD=1&RTy=0&RC=1&RP=1&RA=0&y=18&th=0.

Clarkson, Stephen, and Christina McCall. *Trudeau and Our Times, Volume 1: The Magnificent Obsession* (Toronto: McClelland & Stewart, 1990), and *Volume 2: The Heroic Delusion* (Toronto: McClelland & Stewart, 1994).

Cohen, Andrew, and J.L. Granatstein, eds. *Trudeau's Shadow: The Life and Legacy of Pierre Elliott Trudeau* (Toronto: Vintage Canada, 1999).

Couture, Claude. *Paddling With the Current: Pierre Elliott Trudeau, Étienne Parent, Liberalism, and Nationalism in Canada.* Trans. Vivien Bosley (Edmonton: University of Alberta Press, 1998).

Craig, Brenda, Craig Oliver and Ian McLeod, prods. & wrs. Documentary. *Pierre Trudeau: A Canadian Affair*. (McIntyre Media, 1999).

Dufour, Christian. *A Canadian Challenge / Le défi québécois* (Lantzville, BC: Oolichan Books, 1990).

English, John. *Citizen of the World: The Life of Pierre Elliott Trudeau, Volume One: 1919–1968* (Toronto: Knopf, 2006).

———, Richard Gwyn and P. Whitney Lackenbauer, eds. *The Hidden Pierre Elliott Trudeau: The Faith Behind the Politics* (Ottawa: Novalis, 2004).

Grigsby, Wayne, wr., and Jerry Ciccoritti, dir. Drama. *Trudeau* (Big Motion Pictures, 2002).

———, wr., and Tim Southam, dir. Drama. *Trudeau II: Maverick in the Making* (Double Shoot Productions, 2004).

Gwyn, Richard. *The Northern Magus*. (Toronto: McClelland & Stewart, 1980).

Kidder, Margot. Personal Interview. September 3, 2008.

Laforest, Guy. *Trudeau and the End of the Canadian Dream*. Trans. Paul Leduc Browne & Michelle Weinroth (Montreal: McGill-Queen's University Press, 1995).

Lalonde, Marc. Personal Interview. July 17, 2008 and August 4, 2008.

Lévesque, René. *Memoirs*. Trans. Philip Stratford (Toronto: McClelland & Stewart, 1995).

McKenna, Brian, dir. Documentary. *Pierre Elliott Trudeau: Memoirs, Volumes 1–3* (Les Productions La Fête, 1994).

McKenna, Terence, dir. & wr. Documentary. *Black October* (Canadian Broadcasting Corporation, 2000).

Nemni, Max and Monique. *Young Trudeau, 1919–1944: Son of Quebec, Father of Canada.* Trans. William Johnson (Toronto: McClelland & Stewart, 2006).

Pelletier, Gérard. *Years of Impatience 1950–1960.* Trans. Alan Brown (Toronto: Methuen, 1984).

——, *Years of Choice, 1960–1968.* Trans. Alan Brown (Toronto: Methuen, 1987).

Radwanski, George. *Trudeau.* (Toronto: Macmillan, 1978).

Roux, Jean-Louis. *Nous sommes tous des acteurs* (Montréal: Éditions Lescop, 1998).

Société Radio-Canada. *Les Archives de Radio-Canada.* Available at: http://archives.radio-canada.ca/recherche?q=Pierre+trudeau& RTy=0&RC=1&RP=1&RD=1&RA=0&th=1&x=13&y=12.

Southam, Nancy, ed. *Pierre: Colleagues and Friends Talk About the Pierre They Knew* (Toronto: McClelland & Stewart, 2005).

Trudeau, Margaret. *Beyond Reason* (New York: Paddington, 1979).

——. *Consequences* (Toronto: McClelland & Stewart, 1982).

Trudeau, Pierre Elliott. *Federalism and the French Canadians* (Toronto: Macmillan, 1968).

——. *Pierre Trudeau Speaks Out on Meech Lake*. Ed. Donald Johnston (Toronto: General Paperbacks, 1990).

——. *Memoirs*. (Toronto: McClelland & Stewart, 1993).

——. *Against the Current: Selected Writings 1939–1996*. Ed. Gérard Pelletier (Toronto: McClelland & Stewart, 1996).

——, comp. & ed. *The Asbestos Strike*. Trans. James Boake (Toronto: James Lewis & Samuel, 1974).

——, and Thomas S. Axworthy, eds. *Towards a Just Society: The Trudeau Years* (Toronto: Penguin, 1992).

——, and Jacques Hébert. *Two Innocents in Red China*. Rev. ed. Intro. Alexandre Trudeau. Trans. I.M. Owen (Vancouver: Douglas & MacIntyre, 2007).

Wright, Robert. *Three Nights in Havana: Pierre Trudeau, Fidel Castro and the Cold War World* (Toronto: Harper Collins, 2007).

ACKNOWLEDGMENTS

First and foremost, I would like to thank John Ralston Saul for trusting me with this project and for guiding me through every stage of it. My thanks also to Diane Turbide at Penguin for her editorial input and support and to David Davidar and everyone at Penguin for the tremendous energy and enthusiasm they have put into this series.

George Galt was my first reader, and I thank him for generously sharing with me his own insights on Trudeau and for saving me from some embarrassing errors. Two lengthy conversations I had with Marc Lalonde were important in deepening my understanding of Trudeau, as was a conversation I had with Margot Kidder. John Fraser was kind enough to allow me access to the University of Toronto's library services for my research. Steven Hayward and Katherine Carlstrom provided both material and moral support. Rowley Mossop and Stephen Henighan gave me sufficient provocation to keep the spectre of my ignorance always before me. Erika de Vasconcelos, as always, bore the brunt of my many inefficiencies. Finally, Bob Jackson and Uli and Thomas Menzefricke provided sanctuary at two critical junctures without which this book may never have been written.

By far my largest debt, however, is to my sources. Given the format of this series and the absence of traditional foot-noting or endnoting, it has not been possible in every instance to credit those sources with the thoroughness usual in more scholarly works. The online digital archives of both the CBC and Radio Canada proved invaluable during my research, providing a sampling of material related to Trudeau that spanned nearly fifty years. Stephen Clarkson and Christina McCall's *Trudeau and Our Times, Volume 1: The Magnificent Obsession* and *Volume 2: The Heroic Delusion* remain central to my understanding of Trudeau, and are very much present in this work. Max and Monique Nemni's *Young Trudeau, 1919–1944: Son of Quebec, Father of Canada* provided me with crucial insight into aspects of Trudeau's formation hitherto largely unknown. Finally, John English's *Citizen of the World: The Life of Pierre Elliott Trudeau, Volume One: 1919–1968* served as my roadmap in my negotiation of the first half of Trudeau's life. In his exhaustive analysis of the Trudeau archives and in his inte-gration of archival material with other existing sources and his own original research, English has set the standard for future work on Trudeau. I am grateful to him for his book and for his generous permission to quote excerpts from it without fee. I am also very grateful to the Trudeau estate for their permission to quote without fee from Trudeau's *Memoirs* and from archival material that appears both in *Citizen of the World* and in *Young Trudeau.*

1919   Joseph Philippe Pierre Yves Elliott Trudeau is born on October 18 in Montreal.

1921   Pierre's father, Charles, gives up his law practice to found a string of service stations he will sell to Imperial Oil in 1932 for $1.2 million.

1932   Trudeau enrols in the new Collège Jean-de-Brébeuf in Montreal.

1935   Charles Trudeau suffers a fatal heart attack while vacationing in Florida.

1940   Trudeau completes his studies at Brébeuf at the top of his class. After failing to win a Rhodes Scholarship, he enters law school at the Université de Montréal.

1942–43 Trudeau takes part in an underground revolutionary sect known as *les X.*

1943   He graduates from law school and completes a year of articling at Hyde & Ahern in Montreal.

1944   Trudeau enrols in a master's program in political studies at Harvard.

1946 After graduating from Harvard, Trudeau works at a gold mine in Abitibi, then begins a year of study at the Sorbonne.

1947 He begins a year of study under Harold Laski at the London School of Economics.

1948 Trudeau embarks on travels that take him through Europe, the Middle East, and the Far East.

1949 After his involvement in the Asbestos Strike, Trudeau is turned down for a teaching job at the Université de Montréal and becomes a junior clerk at the Privy Council Office in Ottawa.

1951 Trudeau quits the civil service and devotes himself to the journal *Cité libre*, founded by him and his friend Gérard Pelletier in 1950.

1956 *Cité libre* publishes *The Asbestos Strike*, a collection of essays edited and introduced by Trudeau.

1960 The June election victory of Jean Lesage's Liberals over the Union Nationale marks the beginning of Quebec's Quiet Revolution.

1962 Trudeau publishes "The New Treason of the Intellectuals," attacking the new Quebec nationalists and their growing separatism.

1965 Trudeau is elected to the federal Liberals, along with friends Gérard Pelletier and Jean Marchand.

1966 He takes a position as Lester Pearson's parliamentary secretary.

1967 Trudeau is appointed justice minister and introduces controversial revisions to the Criminal Code that bring him national prominence.

1968 Trudeaumania carries Trudeau to the Liberal leadership in April. In a June election, Trudeau's Liberals take 154 of 264 seats.

1969 Parliament passes the Official Languages Act, establishing English and French as Canada's official languages.

1970 The FLQ kidnap British trade commissioner James Cross and Quebec labour minister Pierre Laporte from their Montreal homes. Laporte is killed after the Trudeau government invokes the War Measures Act.

1971 Trudeau, aged fifty-one, marries twenty-two-year-old Margaret Sinclair after a secret courtship. On Christmas Day, Margaret gives birth to son Justin. Two more sons will follow, Alexandre ("Sacha"), born

Christmas Day 1973, and Michel ("Micha"), born October 1975.

1972 After a lacklustre campaign, Trudeau's Liberals are re-elected with a slim minority.

1974 The Liberals regain their majority in a July election with the help of "the Margaret factor," taking 141 seats to the Conservatives' 95.

1975 Trudeau introduces wage and price controls to fight inflation after having ridiculed a similar Conservative proposal.

1976 The election of René Lévesque's Parti Québécois raises the spectre of Quebec independence.

1977 Margaret Trudeau's night with the Rolling Stones in Toronto makes international headlines.

1979 Trudeau announces his retirement after Joe Clark's Progressive Conservatives form a minority government, then agrees to return as Liberal leader when the Conservatives bungle a confidence vote.

1980 Trudeau wins another majority, though with no seats west of Manitoba. In May, his promise to Quebecers to renew federalism helps defeat a referendum on sovereignty.

1981 The federal government signs the "Kitchen Accord" with all the provinces except Quebec.

1982 Canada patriates its constitution under the Constitution Act, entrenching within it the Charter of Rights and Freedoms.

1984 Trudeau resigns for the second time. In a September election, the Liberals, under John Turner, suffer the worst defeat in their history, capturing only 40 seats to the 211 of Brian Mulroney's Progressive Conservatives.

1985 Parti Québécois leader René Lévesque resigns. Lévesque will die of a heart attack in 1987.

1987 Brian Mulroney and the ten provincial premiers negotiate the Meech Lake Accord. Trudeau publicly denounces the accord.

1990 The Meech Lake Accord dies after Premier Clyde Wells refuses to put it to a vote in the Newfoundland legislature.

1991 Canadian constitutional lawyer Deborah Coyne gives birth to a daughter by Trudeau, Sarah Elisabeth.

1992 Trudeau speaks out against the Charlottetown Accord, which is subsequently defeated in a national referendum.

1998 Margaret and Pierre's twenty-three-year-old son Michel dies while skiing in the B.C. Rockies.

2000 Trudeau dies on September 28, after battling Parkinson's disease and prostate cancer.